Number 142
Summer 2014

New Directions for Evaluation

Paul R. Brandon
Editor-in-Chief

Revisiting Truth, Beauty, and Justice: Evaluating With Validity in the 21st Century

James C. Griffith
Bianca Montrosse-Moorhead
Editors

Revisiting Truth, Beauty, and Justice: Evaluating With Validity in the 21st Century
James C. Griffith, Bianca Montrosse-Moorhead (eds.)
New Directions for Evaluation, no. 142
Paul R. Brandon, Editor-in-Chief

Microfilm copies of issues and articles are available in 16mm and 35mm, as well as microfiche in 105mm, through University Microfilms Inc., 300 North Zeeb Road, Ann Arbor, MI 48106-1346.

New Directions for Evaluation is indexed in Education Research Complete (EBSCO Publishing), ERIC: Education Resources Information Center (CSC), Higher Education Abstracts (Claremont Graduate University), SCOPUS (Elsevier), Social Services Abstracts (ProQuest), Sociological Abstracts (ProQuest), and Worldwide Political Science Abstracts (ProQuest).

New Directions for Evaluation (ISSN 1097-6736, electronic ISSN 1534-875X) is part of The Jossey-Bass Education Series and is published quarterly by Wiley Subscription Services, Inc., A Wiley Company, at Jossey-Bass, One Montgomery Street, Suite 1200, San Francisco, CA 94104-4594.

Subscriptions for individuals cost $89 for U.S./Canada/Mexico; $113 international. For institutions, $334 U.S.; $374 Canada/Mexico; $408 international. Electronic only: $89 for individuals all regions; $334 for institutions all regions. Print and electronic: $98 for individuals in the U.S., Canada, and Mexico; $122 for individuals for the rest of the world; $387 for institutions in the U.S.; $427 for institutions in Canada and Mexico; $461 for institutions for the rest of the world.

Editorial correspondence should be addressed to the Editor-in-Chief, Paul R. Brandon, University of Hawai'i at Mānoa, 1776 University Avenue, Castle Memorial Hall Rm 118, Honolulu, HI 96822-2463.

www.josseybass.com

Editorial Policy and Procedures

New Directions for Evaluation, a quarterly sourcebook, is an official publication of the American Evaluation Association. The journal publishes works on all aspects of evaluation, with an emphasis on presenting timely and thoughtful reflections on leading-edge issues of evaluation theory, practice, methods, the profession, and the organizational, cultural, and societal context within which evaluation occurs. Each issue of the journal is devoted to a single topic, with contributions solicited, organized, reviewed, and edited by one or more guest editors.

The editor-in-chief is seeking proposals for journal issues from around the globe about topics new to the journal (although topics discussed in the past can be revisited). A diversity of perspectives and creative bridges between evaluation and other disciplines, as well as chapters reporting original empirical research on evaluation, are encouraged. A wide range of topics and substantive domains is appropriate for publication, including evaluative endeavors other than program evaluation; however, the proposed topic must be of interest to a broad evaluation audience. For examples of the types of topics that have been successfully proposed, go to http://www.josseybass.com/WileyCDA/Section/id-155510.html.

Journal issues may take any of several forms. Typically they are presented as a series of related chapters, but they might also be presented as a debate; an account, with critique and commentary, of an exemplary evaluation; a feature-length article followed by brief critical commentaries; or perhaps another form proposed by guest editors.

Submitted proposals must follow the format found via the Association's website at http://www.eval.org/Publications/NDE.asp. Proposals are sent to members of the journal's Editorial Advisory Board and to relevant substantive experts for single-blind peer review. The process may result in acceptance, a recommendation to revise and resubmit, or rejection. The journal does not consider or publish unsolicited single manuscripts.

Before submitting proposals, all parties are asked to contact the editor-in-chief, who is committed to working constructively with potential guest editors to help them develop acceptable proposals. For additional information about the journal, see the "Statement of the Editor-in-Chief" in the Spring 2013 issue (No. 137).

Paul R. Brandon, Editor-in-Chief
University of Hawai'i at Mānoa
College of Education
1776 University Avenue
Castle Memorial Hall, Rm. 118
Honolulu, HI 968222463
e-mail: nde@eval.org

Contents

EDITORS' NOTES

In her invitation to submit proposals for the 2010 annual meeting of the American Evaluation Association (AEA), *Evaluation Quality*, Leslie Cooksy stated, "While we evaluate programs, policies, and other entities as a matter of course, we rarely have the opportunity to reflect on the evaluation of our own work or on the theoretical and practical issues associated with evaluation quality. I hope the 2010 conference will provide that opportunity." As a starting point for the discussion, she proposed we use the standards of quality identified in House's (1980) seminal work, *Evaluating with Validity*, and she went on to identify several questions as bases for discussion. This issue of *New Directions for Evaluation* (NDE) began as a reaction to that invitation.

Excited by this theme and the opportunity to engage with House's proposed standards for evaluation validity, the editors of this issue, then serving as the leadership for the Theories of Evaluation Topical Interest Group, proposed a panel discussion aimed at answering one of those questions, "How do we balance dimensions of evaluation quality when they seem in opposition to one another?" In particular, we asked participants to give attention to how values inform this balancing and which dimension they might themselves give priority. Because the panel was well received, and because engaging this question proved fruitful for all of us, we decided to expand the efforts into the current issue. Along the way, we have added two additional questions to the discussion, "What is the role of context in evaluation quality?" included in Cooksy's original invitation, and "What is the role of argument in evaluation?" For all of us, across the questions, the focus is on consideration of the relevance and application for House's view of evaluating with validity in the 21st century.

It is important to distinguish this issue from two recently published issues. Our focus is not only on a validity typology or its *application to*

A number of individuals assisted in the creation of this issue and we would like to take a moment to show our gratitude. Sandra Mathison offered support for the idea and was an encouraging voice in the proposal development process. Paul Brandon has been equally supportive, a helpful sounding board, and incredibly patient. Four contributors to this issue were involved in the original AEA conference panel that sparked the creation of this issue: Katrina Bledsoe, Jane Davidson, Rodney Hopson, and Ernest House. We are thrilled that they stuck with us for the entire journey. In addition, we would like to include a special thank you to Ernest House for his willingness to explore an alterative format for the final chapter in this issue and the time he spent speaking with us about the ideas contained herein. We would also like to thank the chapter contributors who joined this issue after the AEA conference panel: Tarek Azzam, Marthe Hurteau, Bret Levine, Pamela Pokorny, and David D. Williams. Each makes a valuable contribution. Lastly, we owe a huge debt of gratitude to our families for their love, patience, and support.

evaluation, as explored by Chen, Donaldson, and Mark (2011), but also on the validity of the evaluation itself. A valid *evaluation* involves more than a consideration of such typologies. For example, a valid evaluation involves the way we balance and attend to values. Valuing and context play an important role in the issue, but unlike Julnes (2012), we do not focus exclusively on valuing or on its process or policy implications. Values and valuing in this issue are addressed primarily with reference to their role in the validity and quality of evaluation arguments.

To be clear, we are not suggesting, nor do we think House suggests, that these elements of validity—truth, beauty, and justice—represent different values. Rather, consciously or not, values often influence how we view information that falls under each of these elements and the ways in which we privilege one or more of the elements over the others. And, it is not only the values the evaluator brings to the evaluation but also the values of clients and other stakeholders. One important theme emerging from this issue is the way in which views about "the truth" are shaped by values, especially in the sense that values are built into the frames through which we view the world.

Expanding the Concept of Validity

In the 1991 edition of the *Evaluation Thesaurus*, after discussing the concept of validity and the legitimacy of various *types* of validity, Scriven wrote, "Valid *evaluations* are ones that take into account all relevant factors, given the whole context of the evaluation (particularly including the client's needs) and weight them appropriately in the synthesis process" (p. 372, emphasis ours). In apparent contrast, in the final chapter of a recent NDE issue discussing validity in outcome evaluation as it relates to the Campbellian typology, Shadish (2011) noted, "Validity may be essential to good outcome evaluation, but it is not clear that everything essential to good outcome evaluation needs to be placed into a validity typology" (p. 108). While we agree with both claims, the apparent conflict between them raises a distinction that is important to note.

Consider that while Scriven speaks of the validity *of evaluation*, Shadish comments on the essential nature of validity *to evaluation*. Scriven claims that an evaluation's validity depends upon its consideration of "*all* relevant factors, given the *whole context* of the evaluation." Shadish suggests that *not everything* essential to *good* evaluation "needs to be placed into a validity typology." Shadish and Scriven appear to be referring to *validity* in different senses. A consideration of House's treatment of validity clarifies what are these different senses.

In *Evaluating with Validity*, House presents a definition of validity quite compatible with the one Scriven later includes in the *Evaluation Thesaurus*.

Specifically, in the final chapter of that book, House (1980) writes, "In a broad sense, I take validity to mean something like 'worthiness of being recognized'" (p. 249). He continues,

> The dictionary definition is, "the quality of being well-founded on fact, or established on sound principles, and thoroughly applicable to the case or circumstances; soundness and strength (of argument, proof, authority, etc.)" (*OED*). The concept of validity that I have applied to evaluation is considerably expanded from the traditional notion of *validity as prediction*, although inclusive of it.... The modern practice of [program] evaluation is properly seen as a social decision procedure. (p. 249)

House here makes a distinction between validity of evaluation and validity as prediction. In the context of that chapter and especially the three chapters in Part II of the book (Standards for Evaluation—Truth, Beauty, and Justice), he appears to intend an even wider distinction. Predictive validity is presented as only part of validity as it pertains to accuracy of statement or getting the facts right. House writes,

> In the narrow sense of quantitative objectivity, validity is equated with prediction—with checking the data against a criterion. But that assumes a single intent and assumes intersubjectivism as the verification principle. This is too narrow a procedure. Ultimately, says Cronbach (1971), validity is dependent on how the data are to be used and "utility depends upon values, not upon the statistical connections of scores." (p. 89)

So there is more to getting the facts right than predictive validity. And House (2011) further clarifies his view that there is more to evaluative validity than getting the facts right: "As my colleagues in this issue note, Campbell and Stanley's typology is a conception of experimental [predictive] validity, not of evaluation. However ... these validity discussions influence evaluations employing experimental methods" (p. 71).

The sense of validity House applies to evaluation is the more general sense of argumentative validity, within which other, narrower senses of validity, like predictive validity, play a role in establishing the validity of each of the major supporting claims for the argument. These narrower senses play a role in, rather than constituting the whole of, the validity of the supporting claims because, in truth, even these senses of validity are applied to arguments rather than tests, measures, or research designs, including experiments. This is not a controversial or minority view, but one supported by the primary parties in debates about the proper view of validity typologies. Shadish, Cook, and Campbell (2001) define *validity* as "the truth of, correctness of, or degree of support for an inference" (p. 513). Similarly, in their edited volume on test validity, Wainer and Braun (1988) state, "Validity, however, is a unitary concept. Although evidence may be accumulated in many ways, validity always refers to the degree to which that evidence supports the inferences that are made from the test scores" (p. xvii). While it is not the focus of this issue of NDE, some in these debates argue for the inclusion of context and values in even these narrower senses of validity (Cronbach, 1988; Wainer & Braun, 1988).

As already noted, House (1980) promotes a view of evaluation as a "social decision procedure" (p. 249). "One must take seriously the opinions of other people and engage them in serious discourse. This is the realm of argumentation and the proper sphere of evaluation" (House, 1980, p. 94). A useful way of thinking about what this means for evaluation is that there is a moral imperative that the arguments and their conclusions reflect the way things are. At the same time, there is a pragmatic imperative that the arguments be persuasive. It is not uncommon in the public arena for arguments that meet the latter imperative to win out over arguments that meet the former imperative. As evaluation professionals in a position to serve as change agents then, we have an ethical obligation to build arguments that meet both imperatives, lest the true lose to the convincing. In this broader sense of evaluation as argumentation, House identifies the three major dimensions of the validity of evaluative arguments as truth, beauty, and justice. "In summary, then, the validity of an evaluation depends upon whether the evaluation is true, credible, and normatively correct" (House, 1980, p. 255).

Clarity and Disclosure Regarding the Terms of Evaluating With Validity

For the sake of clarity, we should make a further distinction regarding validity. As we have said, the focus here is on the validity of evaluation arguments. In contemporary philosophical reasoning, and in logic, validity is a property that applies only to entirely deductive arguments. In that context, an argument is valid when the truth of its premises (reasons offered in support of the conclusion) guarantees the truth of the conclusion. In other words, in a valid argument, *if* the premises are true, the conclusion *must* be true. We are not employing this strict sense of "validity" here. In evaluation, we are not dealing with conclusions that can be guaranteed to be true. Indeed, most arguments with practical significance involve inductive properties.

As Scriven (1991) points out, logicians did not coin the term *valid* and the earliest uses of the term did not refer to inferences (*Oxford English Dictionary*). Early uses of *valid* applied to inferences did not carry the technical meaning as applied in logic today. In the context of arguments, proof, and assertions, the *OED* currently defines *valid* as "well founded and fully applicable to the particular matter or circumstances; sound and to the point; against which no objection can fairly be brought." This is the sense in which *valid* and *validity* are employed in this issue and in *Evaluating with Validity*. We and House are not alone in this usage. As already noted, Cronbach and others implicitly endorse this usage when they acknowledge that the various forms of validity in the validity typologies apply to [inductive] inferences and particular contexts and not to individual tests, experiments, or measures (Cronbach, 1988; Shadish et al., 2001; Wainer & Braun, 1988).

We should clarify also the use of some of the terms in the discussion of validity. In particular, it will be helpful for the reader to understand House's, and consequently this issue's, use of *truth*, *beauty*, and *justice*—the terms used for the three dimensions essential for evaluating with validity. The intended meanings of these terms and the development of House's use of them are further covered in Chapters 1 and 8, but we will comment briefly on them here.

The first dimension might be said to encompass the narrower senses of validity, particularly those concerned with getting the facts right and the individual premises to which they apply. For House, truth and validity, while not identical, are very closely related. This again is in agreement with the Campbellian tradition (Cook & Campbell, 1979; Shadish et al., 2001) as the major contributors use them almost interchangeably—"We shall use the concepts *validity* and *invalidity* to refer to the best available approximation to the truth or falsity of propositions, including propositions about cause" (Cook & Campbell, 1979, p. 37, emphasis in original). Consistent with a nondeductive use of *validity*, Cook and Campbell continue, "In keeping with the discussion in chapter 1, we should always use the modifier 'approximately' when referring to validity, since one can never know what is true. At best, one can know what has not yet been ruled out as false" (p. 37).

For House, this is especially applicable to evaluation. He argues that if certainty is unachievable, then the goal is to achieve credibility and to persuade rationally. These ideas presuppose an audience and a need "to take their concerns seriously" (House, 1980, p. 74), but

> It is not uncommon for the evaluator to muster information appropriate to an audience of psychologists but which has little meaning for a teacher or a government official.... Evaluation techniques are often presented as being nonargumentative, as, for example, being based on valid and reliable instruments, as employing sound statistical procedures, and so on. In fact, all statements made on the basis of an evaluation are subject to challenge and are arguable—if properly challenged. The more technical and quantitative the evaluation, the less a naïve audience will be able to challenge it, and the evaluation will appear to be more certain than it is. (p. 74)

In a sense, to present evaluation results in this way is to mask the truth, to conceal its weaknesses from our audience. This is not always intentional, or even conscious, but it is an element to which a valid evaluation will attend. This is an important part of why "beauty" is also a key component to validity.

NEW DIRECTIONS FOR EVALUATION • DOI: 10.1002/ev

Beauty, the second dimension, is usefully understood as the way in which each of these premises is presented and the way in which they are presented and organized as a whole. In *Evaluating with Validity*, House uses *coherence* and *credibility* to refer to *beauty*, or the aesthetics of evaluation argument. Aesthetics are more than mere window dressing for House. If, in striving for *truth*, we aim at credibility by identifying, taking seriously, and addressing ourselves to the appropriate audience and providing evidence acceptable to that audience, then in striving for *beauty*, we aim at credibility by presenting the evidence in terms that have meaning for that audience, by setting the claims in contexts relevant to that audience, and by allowing their values to influence the framing of the evaluation and the questions it answers.

Coherence refers to the organization and the "problem-setting stories" within which we situate the premises of an evaluation argument (House, 1980, pp. 101–105). This organization and problem setting is of primary importance. When we collect data, or facts, for an evaluation, problem setting, or framing, has already occurred. This is not to say that we cannot reframe or come to see that another frame makes better sense of the facts; the point is that we need the framing for the facts to be coherent. Facts without context are virtually meaningless. As Ernie states in the interview for Chapter 8,

> Human beings make sense of stuff by framing stuff. You can't make sense out of it without framing it. Making sense out of it means framing it. But, you can use frames which are better, and you can use frames which are worse. That's the idea. And that's where you get into coherence and credibility.

This is one place in which the values of the evaluator and the stakeholders enter evaluations; values are built into the frames through which we view the world. In this way, truth and beauty are intertwined because truth is situated within these frames and at least some "truths" are relative to these frames. Perhaps more fundamentally, these frames determine the questions for which it is important to seek true answers.

Finally, another dimension of validity, and often at least an implicit major premise of an evaluation, relates to the sense of justice to which the evaluator subscribes and is thus reflected in the evaluation (House, 1980, pp. 119–121). Two major issues confronting the justice of an evaluation are voice and representation—whose voices are heard and how are they represented? As House states, referring to an educational setting and summarizing a discussion of how different measures and stakeholder views might be employed, "How the interests of the student are represented in the evaluation, and whose interests are registered will result in significantly different evaluations" (p. 121).

Brief Overview of Chapters

The issue opens with a chapter by Ernest R. House in which he outlines the origin of the validity dimensions he proposes, drawing special attention to contextual influences, and situates his dimensions in the present context. In Chapter 2, James C. Griffith and Bianca Montrosse-Moorhead, through the use of case examples, attempt to illustrate how House's dimensions operate in differing evaluation contexts, and highlight the dilemmas evaluation practitioners face in balancing the priorities between these three dimensions when they conflict. In Chapter 3, E. Jane Davidson draws our attention to the fact that one of the most important aspects of investigation and subsequent presentation of arguments is finding the right questions and then addressing the evaluation to those questions. In Chapter 4, Marthe Hurteau and David D. Williams summarize grounded theory research they have been conducting in both the United States and Canada, present a descriptive model of a process to produce credible evaluation judgments, and argue that their model provides descriptive evidence to support House's vision of validity. In Chapter 5, Tarek Azzam and Bret Levine extend House's work on credibility with the political context and introduce two new ideas—political credibility and politically responsive evaluation. In Chapter 6, Katrina L. Bledsoe shows us how justice in evaluation can play out in community-based evaluations and how attention to those views will go a long way toward understanding stakeholders with values and conceptual frames that may differ from our own. In Chapter 7, Rodney K. Hopson uses House's justice dimension as the foundation for advancing notions of power, fairness, justice, and rights in both formal evaluation theory and practice. In the final chapter, Bianca Montrosse-Moorhead, James C. Griffith, and Pamela Pokorny present a summary and analysis of the entire issue, grounded in both the chapters presented in this issue and a series of formal conversations between the issue editors and Ernest R. House, as a means to assess the current state and vision forward concerning the validity of evaluative arguments.

Revisiting House's ideas with colleagues has been both enjoyable and fruitful, yielding new ways for engaging familiar ideas. After you spend some time with us in the ensuing chapters, we hope you will agree that the ideas presented in House's original work, *Evaluating with Validity*, extend well into the future 21st century.

References

Chen, H. T., Donaldson, S. I., & Mark, M. M. (Eds.). (2011). *New Directions for Evaluation: No. 130. Advancing validity in outcome evaluation: Theory and practice.* San Francisco, CA: Jossey-Bass

Cook, T. D., & Campbell, D. T. (1979). *Quasi-experimentation: Design and analysis issues for field settings.* Boston, MA: Houghton Mifflin.

Cooksy, L. J. (2010). Call for proposals & presidential invitation. Retrieved from http://archive.eval.org/eval2010/10cfp.htm

Cronbach, L. J. (1988). Five perspectives on validity argument. In H. Wainer & H. Braun (Eds.), *Test validity* (pp. 3–17). Hillsdale, NJ: Lawrence Erlbaum.

House, E. R. (1980). *Evaluating with validity.* Beverly Hills, CA: Sage

House, E. R. (2011). Conflict of interest and Campbellian validity. In H. T. Chen, S. I. Donaldson, & M. M. Mark (Eds.), *New Directions for Evaluation: No. 130. Advancing validity in outcome evaluation: Theory and practice* (pp. 69–80). San Francisco, CA: Jossey-Bass. doi:10.1002/ev.366

Julnes, G. (Ed.). (2012). *New Directions for Evaluation: No. 133. Promoting valuation in the public interest: Informing policies for judging value in evaluation.* San Francisco, CA: Jossey-Bass.

Scriven, M. (1991). *Evaluation thesaurus* (4th ed.). Newbury Park, CA: Sage.

Shadish, W. R. (2011). The truth about validity. In H. T. Chen, S. I. Donaldson, & M. M. Mark (Eds.), *New Directions for Evaluation: No. 130. Advancing validity in outcome evaluation: Theory and practice* (pp. 107–117). San Francisco, CA: Jossey-Bass. doi:10.1002/ev.369

Shadish, W. R., Cook, T. D., & Campbell, D. T. (2001). *Experimental and quasi-experimental designs for generalized causal inference.* Boston, MA: Houghton Mifflin.

Wainer, H., & Braun, H. (Eds.). (1988). *Test validity.* Hillsdale, NJ: Lawrence Erlbaum.

James C. Griffith
Bianca Montrosse-Moorhead
Editors

JAMES C. GRIFFITH *is a doctoral candidate for a dual degree in philosophy and psychology at the Claremont Graduate University and a lead evaluator at the Claremont Evaluation Center.*

BIANCA MONTROSSE-MOORHEAD *is an assistant professor in the Measurement, Evaluation and Assessment program, a research scientist for the Collaborative on Strategic Education Reform (CSER), and coordinator of the Graduate Certificate Program in Program Evaluation at the University of Connecticut.*

House, E. R. (2014). Origins of the ideas in *Evaluating with Validity*. In J. C. Griffith & B. Montrosse-Moorhead (Eds.), *Revisiting truth, beauty, and justice: Evaluating with validity in the 21st century. New Directions for Evaluation, 142*, 9–15.

1

Origins of the Ideas in *Evaluating with Validity*

Ernest R. House

Abstract

The book Evaluating with Validity *(House, 1980) broadened the evaluation field's conception of validity by contending that evaluations should be true, coherent, and just. Untrue, incoherent, and unjust evaluations are invalid. The working ideas were argument, coherence, and politics. Truth is the attainment of arguments soundly made, beauty is the attainment of coherence well wrought, and justice is the attainment of politics fairly done. For the truth criterion, it wasn't designs or correlations that determined validity, but rather the validity of the arguments that supported the use of the designs and correlations. The broader conception of validity grew from addressing problems encountered in conducting evaluations. This chapter traces the origins of the ideas and the social context from which they emerged. It contends that these criteria still apply, though the contents of the criteria have changed somewhat and the context has changed substantially.* © Wiley Periodicals, Inc., and the American Evaluation Association.

When Leslie Cooksy, president of the American Evaluation Association, announced that the theme of the 2010 annual conference would be the quality of evaluations, she cited my *Evaluating with Validity* book on truth, beauty, and justice in evaluation (House, 1980). It's rare to cite a particular work in announcing the conference theme, and several people have asked me where the original ideas came from.

NEW DIRECTIONS FOR EVALUATION, no. 142, Summer 2014 © Wiley Periodicals, Inc., and the American Evaluation Association. Published online in Wiley Online Library (wileyonlinelibrary.com) • DOI: 10.1002/ev.20081

In the book I tried to broaden the field's conception of validity. At the time, validity was associated with Campbell and Stanley's (1966) analysis of experimental and quasi-experimental studies. They posited internal and external validities and argued that various experimental designs could address potential biases. They further argued that when biases are addressed the findings are valid. Another common notion of validity put forth by Cronbach and Meehl (1955) was that the correlation between the scores of tests, presumably measuring the same underlying construct, indicated their validity.

Put simply, my broadening of the concept of validity was based on the idea that if an evaluation is untrue, or incoherent, or unjust, it is invalid. In other words, an evaluation must be true, coherent, and just. All three criteria are necessary. By contrast, sound fiscal judgment is not necessary to establish evaluation validity, that is, if an evaluation is expensive, that doesn't make its findings invalid. To add some flair, I talked about "truth, beauty, and justice" in evaluation. The underlying concepts were argument, coherence, and politics. Truth is the *attainment* of arguments soundly made, beauty is the *attainment* of coherence well wrought, and justice is the *attainment* of politics fairly done.

For the truth criterion, I contended that it wasn't the designs or correlations that determined validity, but rather the validity of the arguments that supported the use of these designs. All validity types necessarily rely on supporting arguments. My analysis was consistent with later developments in informal and probative logic (Scriven, 2012). Broadening the validity concept doesn't replace other conceptions, but rather focuses on the arguments that all must depend on. Following this logic, I also contended that qualitative evaluations could be valid, depending on the arguments made for them.

Of course, these criteria are ideals. We can never have a perfectly true, coherent, or just evaluation. Attainment is a matter of degree. However, we can often recognize when evaluations are so far awry that we consider them untrue, incoherent, or unjust. Although I've presented the ideas here as if conceived in a flash of insight, that's not how they evolved. They grew gradually from concrete experiences. I'll recount the origins of the ideas, discuss how they've changed, and consider whether they are still relevant.

The book was based on my early evaluation experiences and grew organically from the center outward, a piece at a time as I encountered specific problems. I began a career in 1967 with a large-scale, four-year evaluation of the Illinois Gifted Education Program. To prepare, I read the evaluation literature in a month. There wasn't much. My experiences in the Illinois study convinced me that evaluation was highly political, not a common idea at the time. In fact, I asked myself, "Is it all politics?"

The possibility that it might be all politics bothered me. Surely, there must be a way to adjudicate what evaluators did. About that time I saw a review of John Rawls' *A Theory of Justice* (1971). Maybe this was what I needed. If politics were about who got what, an ethical framework might help. After reading Rawls, I wrote "Justice in Evaluation" in 1975. Given that justice is so much a part of the discipline's identity presently, it's difficult to imagine the incredulity of people in the field. What could justice possibly have to do with evaluation? The two terms didn't belong in the same sentence. Some did see the relevance. Don Campbell sent for a few dozen mimeo copies, and Gene Glass included the paper in the first *Evaluation Studies Review Annual* (House, 1976). Although I have done many things in the field, the link to social justice has identified me since that time.

During the 1970s the quantitative–qualitative debate also heated up. Along with others, I defended the legitimacy of qualitative studies, the basic issue. Again, I looked for a broader perspective. I saw a review of a book updating the discipline of classic rhetoric as argumentation (Perelman & Olbrechts-Tyteca, 1969). I advanced the notion that evaluations were arguments in which evaluators presented evidence for and against, and that in making such arguments they might use both quantitative and qualitative data. Evaluation was more than research methods. I wrote the "logic of evaluative argument" monograph in 1976 (House, 1977). These ideas gained quick acceptance. I received personal messages from Lee Cronbach and Egon Guba that the monograph had changed their way of thinking. Cronbach recast the validation of standardized tests as arguments, and Guba pushed the concept of "naturalistic evaluation" further in work he and Yvonna Lincoln did later.

Meanwhile, our center at the University of Illinois, led by Tom Hastings and Bob Stake, had begun considering evaluative case studies, influenced by Barry MacDonald and the group at East Anglia. In the Illinois evaluation, my team had collected 40 different kinds of information on a stratified random sample of local gifted programs. How could we pull all these data together? I had used Stake's Countenance model to plan the evaluation, and Bob encouraged us in combining these data into "portrayals." Combining so many different kinds of information into case studies was no small task. In fact, some early attempts were incoherent. Data don't assemble and interpret themselves.

This time the broader framework was to see written evaluation reports as utilizing voice, plot, story, imagery, metaphor, and other framing elements to achieve coherence. I applied these concepts to both case studies and regular scientific studies (House, 1979). One example was Gusfield's (1976) analysis of drunk driving research that demonstrated how these studies changed the image of drinking drivers from social drinkers who have one drink too many to the image of falling down habitual drunks. The shift in image prompted strong legislation. Imagery and other framing devices that convey compacted values I called "the vocabulary of action."

By this time the field of evaluation was expanding rapidly. There were at least 50 different evaluation models. In examining these models, I could see that there were only a few basic approaches. Most models were similar but with different names. To clarify the situation, in *Evaluating with Validity*, I posited that there were eight basic approaches to evaluation and analyzed how these approaches differed from one another in their assumptions, methods, philosophy, and import.

It was one more step to critique both the approaches and government policies of the time with the criteria—metaevaluation. I included these papers in *Evaluating with Validity*, generalizing that truth, beauty, and justice were three broad criteria by which evaluations might be judged. Evaluations should be true, coherent, and just. Untrue, incoherent, and unjust evaluations are invalid. Other chapters extended the principles of fairness and justice through democratizing evaluation, deliberation, and fair evaluation agreements.

In developing each concept, I encountered a practical problem and turned to other disciplines, including philosophy, political science, sociology, psychology, cognitive science, rhetoric, literary theory, and economics, to provide insights. This is one way that evaluation theory develops. You need the practical problem to realize what might be useful. Looking at these ideas together, I generalized to the broader conception of validity.

Thirty Years Later

As it happened, *Evaluating with Validity* was published the year Reagan was elected president. Reagan began dismantling the New Deal and Great Society programs, the core of American social legislation since the 1930s. In their place he promoted deregulation, privatization, and reduced government authority. Succeeding administrations have continued these trends. The new policies transformed society, often in ways never anticipated. For example, the country is still coping with the aftermath of its worst financial crisis since the 1930s, caused in large part by financial deregulation. At its core, evaluation is the same as it was in 1980, but the social context in which it operates has changed.

How relevant are the original validity concepts today? The three broad criteria are still relevant, but the content and applications have shifted somewhat. For example, a major threat facing evaluation is evaluator conflict of interest. Drug companies have gained control of many aspects of drug evaluations, from study design and data analysis to publication. There are a dozen ways in which drug evaluations have been manipulated to produce findings favorable to the companies, which stand to make billions of dollars on the basis of study results (House, 2008).

Some of these studies are invalid in that they produce findings that are incorrect. For a long time, the basic argument legitimating their validity has been that the studies are randomized, double-blinded, combined in meta-analyses, and approved by FDA committees. Unfortunately, although this argument might have been sufficient before, it's inadequate now. Companies have found ways to meet technical standards while biasing findings, such as suppressing negative results, publishing data selectively, censoring what they provide to data banks, and paying large consulting fees to those serving on FDA approval committees.

In these circumstances the arguments for validity via technical adequacy fall short. Even if these particular loopholes were closed, which they should be, there are other ways companies can bias findings. A different argument for bolstering validity would be to reduce evaluator biases directly. That is, it may be more effective to eliminate the opportunity and motivation to manipulate findings than trying to fix biases after the fact. We need to consider evaluator biases at the beginning of the study as well as afterword. That the study be true is still relevant, and we still necessarily depend on arguments to establish validity, but the particular arguments to ensure validity have shifted.

The biased drug studies are also unjust. It's possible to have untrue studies that damage patients inadvertently, such as because of a coding error. I would not call such studies unjust. However, that's not the case with biased drug evaluations. These studies damage unsuspecting patients who have been led to believe the drugs are beneficial to their health. Large numbers of vulnerable people suffer ill effects in order for large profits to accrue to a few. Those disadvantaged in health are victimized. I call such biased evaluations unjust.

Finally, these drug studies are presented in the voice and image of the objective scientist, with accompanying symbols of assurance. A man in a white coat steps forward and says, "Trust me, I'm a medical scientist." The studies are backed with meta-analysis and approved by the FDA (which to its credit has taken steps to remedy the situation). I would call such representations inauthentic. They play on reassuring images to mislead patients. I hasten to add that not all sponsors engage in deceptive practices, but deception is far too common. Unfortunately, biased evaluations are becoming more common in other areas as well, partly as a result of privatization and deregulation.

Hence, although truth, beauty, and justice still serve as criteria for evaluation quality, the content of these criteria has changed. Evaluation still involves making arguments using quantitative and qualitative data, but the nature of the argument has shifted. Ensuring valid evaluations may require examining evaluator conflicts of interest.

Our conception of justice has also shifted. In Rawls' framework, impartial experts judge what is just based on fundamental principles. Minorities and feminists have challenged this stand-apart conception of justice. The idea that participants can express their own views, values, and interests has supplemented, and in some cases supplanted, the idea of impartial judges. Hence, we have participatory evaluations, including deliberative democratic evaluations. Again, justice applies as a criterion, but what we mean by justice has shifted.

Finally, there is the beauty criterion. This is the least understood, perhaps because it is so close to us. The underlying concept is coherence. In the original paper, I illustrated that language, voice, images, metaphors, and points of view are critical in evaluations. These are not merely cosmetic; they can convey the meaning of the study. For example, the image of drinking drivers as falling down drunks led to strong legislation. A critical issue is whether the findings justify that powerful image.

Later I demonstrated that Rossi, Freeman, and Wright's (1979) evaluation textbook was based on an extended metaphor of social programs being industrial pipelines, with attendant outcomes and criteria shaped accordingly (House, 1983). Such metaphors provide coherence and direction to evaluations, sometimes without evaluators being aware. Again, the issue is whether the metaphors and other framing devices are appropriate. An inappropriate framework can lead to incorrect findings. For example, the frame for the evaluation of Jesse Jackson's PUSH/Excel program was that educational programs should be tightly articulated entities with precisely defined inputs and outputs (House, 1988). PUSH/Excel was more like a motivational church program aimed at rousing students to action. Such programs can be evaluated, but on their own terms.

The wrong frame has evaluators looking for the wrong things. Cognitive scientists tell us that we need such frames to interpret events. We have no choice. We necessarily think about the world in terms of stories and causes (Kahneman, 2011). Frames enable us to interpret events coherently and meaningfully. That's how our minds are structured. At the same time, inappropriate framing is a major source of cognitive bias. That's true for evaluations as well. We have work to do to understand our own (often implicit) frameworks.

Until I looked back at these ideas after all these years, I didn't realize how connected they were to my current thinking. Those of us who write a lot about evaluation have only a few themes that we address time and time again in different ways. I apologize for the dated parts of the book, the politically incorrect usage of the time, and the intemperate remarks. Written works bear the mark of their time, place, and maker.

References

Campbell, D., & Stanley, J. (1966). *Experimental and quasi-experimental designs for research*. Chicago, IL: Rand McNally.

Cronbach, L., & Meehl, P. E. (1955). Construct validity in psychological tests. *Psychological Bulletin, 52*, 281–302. doi:10.1037/h0040957

Gusfield, J. (1976). The literary rhetoric of science. *American Sociological Review, 41*, 16–34. doi:10.2307/2094370

House, E. R. (1976). Justice in evaluation. In G. V. Glass (Ed.), *Evaluation studies review annual* (Vol. 1, pp. 75–100). Beverly Hills, CA: Sage.

House, E. R. (1977). The logic of evaluative argument. *Center for the Study of Evaluation Monograph Series, 7*.

House, E. R. (1979). Coherence and credibility: The aesthetics of evaluation. *Educational Evaluation and Policy Analysis, 1*, 5–17. doi:10.3102/01623737001005005

House, E. R. (1980). *Evaluating with validity.* Beverly Hills, CA: Sage. Reissued by Information Age Publications, NC, 2008.

House, E. R. (1983). How we think about evaluation. In E. R. House (Ed.), *New Directions for Program Evaluation: No. 19. Philosophy of evaluation* (pp. 5–25). San Francisco, CA: Jossey-Bass. doi:10.1002/ev.1342

House, E. R. (2008). Blowback: Consequences of evaluation for evaluation. *American Journal of Evaluation, 29,* 416–426. doi:10.1177/1098214008322640

Kahneman, D. (2011). *Thinking fast and slow.* Cambridge, MA: Harvard University Press.

Perelman, C., & Olbrechts-Tyteca, L. (1969). *The new rhetoric: A treatise on argumentation.* Notre Dame, IN: University of Notre Dame Press.

Rawls, J. (1971). *A theory of justice.* Cambridge, MA: Harvard University Press.

Rossi, P. H., Freeman, H. E., & Wright, S. R. (1979). *Evaluation: A systematic approach.* Beverly Hills, CA: Sage.

Scriven, M. (2012). The logic of valuing. In G. Julnes (Ed.), *New Directions for Evaluation: No. 133. Promoting valuing in the public interest: Informing policies for judging value in evaluations* (pp. 17–28). San Francisco, CA: Jossey-Bass. doi:10.1002/ev.20003

ERNEST R. HOUSE *is a professor emeritus of education at the University of Colorado at Boulder.*

Griffith, J. C., & Montrosse-Moorhead, B. (2014). The value in validity. In J. C. Griffith & B. Montrosse-Moorhead (Eds.), *Revisiting truth, beauty, and justice: Evaluating with validity in the 21st century. New Directions for Evaluation, 142*, 17–30.

2

The Value in Validity

James C. Griffith, Bianca Montrosse-Moorhead

Abstract

House's classic Evaluating with Validity *proposes three dimensions—truth, justice, and beauty—for evaluation validity. A challenge to achieving validity is balancing the priorities between these three dimensions when they conflict. This chapter examines the concept of validity and the values inherent in each of these dimensions and any choices between them. Our analysis of these inherent values and any prioritization between truth, justice, and beauty aims to help the evaluator confront the kinds of dilemmas faced when one's commitment to values, evaluation theories, or methodology comes up against conflicting realities for a particular evaluation. Striking an appropriate balance can be particularly challenging in contexts involving diverse cultures or even homogenous cultures of which the evaluator is not a part. We use two case examples to explore the issues in real-life contexts. © Wiley Periodicals, Inc., and the American Evaluation Association.*

Perhaps the most dangerous threat to the validity of an evaluation is a poor understanding of what validity is, to what that approbation applies, or what role values play in striving for validity. Validity is most often discussed in the literature as applicable to measurement and research design (Cronbach & Meehl, 1955; Shadish, Cook, & Campbell, 2001). In particular, there is a robust literature on which research designs are most, and which are least, capable of eliminating threats to validity (Campbell & Stanley, 1966; Chen, Donaldson, Mark, 2011; Collins, Hall, & Paul, 2004;

Cook & Campbell, 1979; Morgan & Winship, 2007; Murnane & Willett, 2010; Scriven, 1976; Shadish, 2011; Shadish et al., 2001). Further literature discusses which types of validity are of most serious concern (Chen et al., 2011; Cronbach, 1982; Shadish et al., 2001). In the context of evaluation, these influential discussions create a dangerous space—one in which "experiment" is so closely tied to discussions about RCTs and particular quasi-experiments, and the concept of validity is so frequently tied to those experiments, that it is all but forgotten that validity is actually a trait of arguments.

Tests and research designs are not valid in the abstract—they are not universally valid. A particular test or research design is suitable for a particular purpose and in a particular context. That is to say, a test or research design is valid insomuch as it contributes to the validity of the argument supporting the claim it is intended to support (Cook & Campbell, 1979; Shadish et al., 2001; Wainer & Braun, 1988). It is arguments that are valid or invalid, and arguments are often about more than a design or a use of a particular method. Further, arguments that have the support of privileged research designs are *not necessarily* better supported than arguments supported by other premises. The important issue is to address and, hopefully, eliminate threats to validity.

Proofs and formal logic aside, arguments in the real world are subject to values in a variety of ways. When we construct arguments for ourselves, there may be fewer values involved and we need not always attend to them. When an argument is constructed for an audience, values require our attention, and a balancing of values is almost always required. Epistemological or methodological values are reflected when we prioritize particular research designs. This is not necessarily problematic, but it can become a problem when the preference is blind or the one preferring is not aware that it is indeed a preference, an expression of value. In such cases, evaluators may not be aware of relevant and suitable alternatives. For example, part of the problem with a policy that prioritizes a particular design is that the policy places accountability for validity almost entirely on research design and often privileges certain aspects of that research design over others. What about the validity of the needs assessment, of the measures being used, or of the formation of the evaluation questions? Constructing an experimental design eliminates various threats to internal validity, but this can give a false sense of confidence in the findings and in the ability of the measures used to generate findings worth having. The validity of the measures, for *that* context, is assumed. Or, at the very least, we are not accustomed to seeing most evaluators make a case for the appropriateness of their measures in the particular evaluative context.

Once it becomes clear that validity is about the validity of the argument supporting claims and that values are inherently intertwined in this process, the evaluator is forced to contemplate how these ideas are present and operate in an evaluative context. House's framing of evaluation validity creates a useful framework within which one can reflect on evaluation decisions before, during, and after key activities have been executed. Both Scriven (1991) and House (1980) take us beyond the narrow focus of validity as it pertains to truth claims about the program. House further points the way by providing a useful lens, or at least presenting us with the fact that there are multiple lenses available, with which we can view what remains of evaluation validity. Neither Scriven nor House tells us precisely what specific factors will be relevant, nor should they. If we take both of them seriously in terms of attending to the entire evaluation context, these factors will vary between evaluations. House has delineated broad factors–dimensions of evaluation validity–and the two case examples included in this chapter will show us how those dimensions come into precise focus. One unavoidable result of such a holistic and comprehensive view of evaluation validity is that there will be, inevitably, instances in which the relevant values come into conflict. As you consider the cases in this chapter, and our analysis of these cases, it will be helpful to keep the following questions in mind:

1. What are the inherent values underlying truth, beauty, and justice and choices about balancing them? What values are we accepting, rejecting, or balancing when we choose between truth, justice, and beauty?
2. How do these dimensions come into conflict in specific evaluation settings and what causes them to do so?
3. How can an evaluator go about appropriately balancing these dimensions to produce valid evaluations? Must the attention to, and weighting of, the dimensions occur only in the final synthesis?

In many ways, the cases in this chapter represent opposite ends on a continuum of contexts in which evaluation practice occurs. Unlike the first case, the second case for analysis focuses on a highly publicized evaluation that ended with much controversy. Unsurprisingly, the evaluation team and other interested parties have written a lot about the case. Additionally, the stakes associated with the evaluation outcomes were much higher in the second case. Lastly, the overall scope of the two cases differs. Yet, both can be used to analyze the central questions we explore in this chapter as a means to better understand the ways in which truth, beauty, and justice operate across evaluation contexts.

Truth, Beauty, and Justice in a Federally Funded Magnet School Evaluation

The current theory of change behind the Magnet Schools Assistance Program (MSAP) is that offering a specialized curriculum attracts students from different social, economic, ethnic, and racial backgrounds.[1] In doing so, magnets reduce minority group isolation while simultaneously improving academic outcomes for all students.

As a means to test this theory of change, and particularly in the context of the particular external evaluation that is the subject of this case, the final evaluation design approved by both the school district and the federal MSAP program was a theory-driven evaluation (Donaldson, 2007) employing a quasi-experimental design. A quasi-experimental design was chosen because of limits imposed upon the external evaluation by the adoption of specific language around "scientifically based evaluation methods." By requiring that the evaluation be consistent with this language, the federal funding agency could ensure that (a) their views about the types of questions that evaluations should answer were prominent and (b) their beliefs about how best to answer those questions were promulgated. Their interests ultimately required that the evaluation team answer the question of whether magnet school attendance led to higher learning gains as measured by state-developed standardized exams for students attending magnet programs compared to those not attending magnet programs. It is also important to note that a quasi-experimental design was chosen over an experimental design because of limits imposed on the external evaluation team by the local program. While they were interested in causal, outcome-oriented questions, they were not interested in them at the expense of denying a potentially successful intervention to students through a random assignment process. This was especially so because the magnet school theory of change states that magnet schools seek to reduce minority group isolation. For the local program staff, the moral imperative of achieving this far out-weighed the benefits of an experimental design.

Further, a theory-driven evaluation design was chosen to meet the related but divergent needs of the local program staff. While they were equally interested in establishing a causal link between magnet school attendance and improved student academic outcomes as measured by state-developed standardized exams, their interest went beyond the simple, "does it work" question. For example, does the magnet program work equally well for all student subgroups? To what extent does school climate appear to influence the degree of effectiveness observed? Their interests ultimately came down to ongoing, formative feedback to inform decision making regarding the schools. Thus, before any evaluation work was conducted, the external evaluation team collaboratively developed a logic model with program staff that depicted the theory of change and hypothesized facilitating and hindering mechanisms.

To meet the demands of "rigor" placed upon the external evaluation team by the federal funding agency, the evaluation staff then delved into the magnet school and school improvement literature to (a) better understand the extant knowledge base regarding the identified facilitating and hindering mechanisms and (b) identify potentially useful surveys and survey items for measuring these domains. The evaluation team chose to modify existing survey instruments to measure potential facilitating and hindering mechanisms within the magnet school context. These survey instruments were pilot-tested, and factor analysis was used to establish the reliability of the instruments used. This process was not only consistent with good survey design, but as a secondary consideration was intended to meet "rigor" demands placed upon the evaluation team by the federal funding agency and therefore increase the likelihood that the results would be perceived as credible. Further, survey administration followed the quasi-experimental design used to assess student outcomes. That is, instruments were administered to students and teachers at the treatment (magnet) and comparison (nonmagnet) schools. Comparison schools were identified using propensity score matching techniques (Parsons, 2001; Rubin, 1997) to comply with the limits imposed on the external evaluation team by the federal funding agency.

The evaluation team had to develop a reporting system that would present the truth as uncovered by the evaluation in a way that would be perceived as credible to multiple stakeholder groups, thus a two-phased reporting system was developed. As a first step, the evaluators produced formal reports using nonacademic language and used a more formal and traditional scientific style for the appendices containing technical information. The intended audience for these briefs was primarily the MSAP grant officer and others in the US Department of Education, and secondarily others interested in a more thorough discussion of results and associated technical details (e.g., researchers and local staff within the district who work daily with accountability data). In addition, findings briefs were created and modeled after state-developed annual testing briefs. These results were disseminated to program staff (including administrators and teachers), students, parents, and board of education members. The evaluation team hypothesized that by modeling the briefs after an existing accountability reporting system within the state, results would be easily digested and therefore more likely to be used. Further, it could capitalize on the perceived credibility of the existing accountability system, further increasing the likelihood of interest in, and use of, findings.

A further important consideration that influenced how the evaluation was conducted and how reports were created and disseminated is that the school district originally hired a different evaluation firm to conduct an external evaluation employing quasi-experimental methods. In the year that followed, the external evaluation contract was terminated for a variety of reasons. For example, that evaluator neglected to involve the local program staff in any portion of the evaluation, including providing progress reports or sharing formative evaluation data. The first official correspondence concerning the projects' progress was a Year-1 summative report that was sent simultaneously to the local program staff and the federal MSAP grant officer. The local program staff read the report and immediately deemed the report uncredible. While the report was coherent in the sense that it was organized by evaluation question, further inspection of data reported in tables and figures was cause for concern. For example, the external evaluator only reported the results for students in one grade level. According to the report,

NEW DIRECTIONS FOR EVALUATION • DOI: 10.1002/ev

this was due to the unavailability of data. This was incongruent with the perspective of the local staff because data on students from multiple grade levels across the district had been sent to the external evaluator. In short, the credibility of the evaluator, and subsequently the findings he or she produced, were called into question. Because the local program staff was very interested in findings that were deemed truthful and credible, the local program staff negotiated with their MSAP grant officer to gain authorization to hire a new evaluation firm. While no concrete evidence exists, one can infer from the MSAP grant officer's approval of this modification that they had similar reservations about the ability for the evaluation to uncover the truth, and as a result, produce credible findings.

The particulars surrounding the context into which the new evaluation team entered also had implications for the proposed evaluation design. In particular, it highlighted that the credibility of evaluation findings would be judged not only on whether the evaluation was uncovering the truth in this particular context, but the role that stakeholder involvement and program staff perceptions played in the perceived credibility of evaluation findings. Specifically, the program staff was sensitive to, and intent on, ensuring that stakeholders were involved in the evaluation process, that findings were grounded in truthful and credible data, and that the team carrying out the external evaluation was not necessarily invested in the success of the program, but were invested in finding answers to evaluation questions. It was not enough for the evaluation to produce truth. Truth had to be produced while being sensitive to local needs and ideas about how evaluation ought to be conducted.

The 1990 National Assessment Governing Board: National Assessment of Educational Progress Standard Setting Evaluation

The National Assessment Governing Board (NAGB) was created in 1988 with the passing of the bill containing the Augustus F. Hawkins–Robert T. Stafford Elementary and Secondary School Improvement Amendments (P.L. 100–297).[2] One of the main responsibilities of the NAGB was to develop and implement a standard-setting process for results from the National Assessment of Educational Progress (NAEP; Vinovskis, 1998). The 1988 School Improvement Amendments also included a mandate requiring an external evaluation of the NAGB standard-setting process. When the NAGB contracted Stufflebeam, Jaeger, and Scriven to conduct the external evaluation shortly after the newly formed standards were released, criticism had already emerged regarding the credibility of the process the NAGB used to set the standards and the proficiency levels based on those standards (Stufflebeam, 2000; Vinovskis, 1998).

NEW DIRECTIONS FOR EVALUATION • DOI: 10.1002/ev

Stufflebeam and his colleagues sought to conduct an evaluation that provided both formative information and an overall summative judgment concerning the reliability and validity of the NAGB process for categorizing students as "below basic," "basic," "proficient," or "advanced" based on their NAEP scores. The evaluation team issued three formative reports which the NAGB used to modify their system. These reports were delivered to NAGB staff and not released for public consumption. In the first report, the evaluators noted significant flaws in the standard-setting process. In the second and third reports, they reported that, despite the NAGB's sincere and constructive attempts to address the concerns and improve the process, significant flaws persisted (Stufflebeam, 2000; Vinovskis, 1998).

Given that the three formative evaluations reported significant flaws and the second and third evaluations reported that attempts to fix the problems had failed, it should come as no surprise that the draft summative report indicated that significant flaws in the standard-setting process remained and that the "resulting standards, which are due to be released in spite of the project's technical failures, must be used only with extreme caution" (Stufflebeam, Jaeger, & Scriven, 1991, as cited in Vinovskis, 1998). The draft was sent out for prerelease review to a total of 45 individuals, representing various stakeholder groups (e.g., NAGB representatives, measurement experts, and policy makers), more than half of which were measurement and research methodology experts. This was done to ensure the report was "sound, clear, useful, and up to the standards Congress would expect" (Stufflebeam, 2000, p. 299). The draft summative report was intended to remain confidential, and those receiving a copy were instructed not to distribute the report because the sole purpose of the prerelease review was to provide feedback for the evaluation team.

Upon receiving the draft summative report and notice that the draft had been disseminated to a prerelease review panel, the NAGB immediately fired Stufflebeam, Jaeger, and Scriven. Further, according to Stufflebeam, the NAGB "sent an unsigned, vitriolic attack on [the] draft report to all members of [the] prerelease review group" (NAGB, 1991; Stufflebeam, 2000, p. 299). Despite being fired, the evaluation team took the recommendations of the non-NAGB prerelease reviewers, incorporated it into the draft, and sent the final summative evaluation report to the NAGB. Why did the evaluation process end on such a bad note? What objections did the NAGB have to the draft summative report?

It seems unlikely that there were serious technical flaws in the draft summative report. That report apparently contained much of what had already been reported in the formative reports without raising objections or criticism from NAGB personnel. In addition, with a few notable exceptions (e.g., Cizek, 1993; Kane, 1993), the many external summative evaluations that ensued after Stufflebeam and colleagues issued their report supported the claims made by Stufflebeam and his colleagues (Linn, Koretz, Barker, &

Burstein, 1991; Shepard, 1993; U.S. General Accounting Office, 1993). So what else explains the acrimonious ending to the evaluative relationship? What happened between the submission of the third formative report and the first draft of the summative report?

Analysis

According to House, it is not uncommon for an evaluator to intensely focus on one dimension of validity to the exclusion of the other two dimensions. He observed that evaluations entrenched in an "objectivist" approach, focus "exclusively on the truth aspect of validity," and are thus "often not credible to those evaluated and are sometimes undemocratic, unfair, or otherwise normatively incorrect" (House 1980, p. 250). We see a clear example of this in the MSAP case when the original evaluator's intense focus on truth prevented him from considering other dimensions of validity, resulting in invalid evaluation conclusions. He was not cognizant of the need to balance the dimensions. The resulting negative evaluation was seen as invalid not only by the program, but by the program officer (the client) the program staff convinced to replace the evaluator. It is not difficult to see why. Based on the description of the original evaluator's approach to the evaluation and relative ambivalence toward relevant stakeholder concerns, we can see that the evaluator would have had a very difficult time producing a valid evaluative argument.

The original evaluator failed to move beyond truth. Intentionally or not, he missed opportunities to learn about his audience and identify common ground that could be used as a foundation for an evaluative argument that might have been accepted by them. Further, the original evaluator did not even communicate with, or identify, the relevant stakeholders, let alone look for ways to give them a voice in the process. Their reaction shows that this deficiency prevented their interests from being represented in the evaluation report to their program officer.

What House does not emphasize, but seems likely, is that such an intense focus on one dimension of validity is a threat to that dimension itself. By ignoring the interests and excluding the voices of the variety of stakeholders, that is, by ignoring beauty and justice, one is likely also to miss at least part of the truth. For example, the original evaluator in the MSAP case not only failed to move *beyond* truth, he even failed on the truth dimension itself, by failing to consider other perspectives or other factors that might influence what was perceived as the truth. Another possibility is not attending to one dimension sufficiently. As we see in the NAGB case, this need not be wholesale neglect and may be the result of factors beyond the evaluator's control. In such cases, the validity of the evaluation, or its degree of validity, may be less clear.

In the NAGB case, privileging truth to the neglect of the other dimensions is not the issue. It is unlikely that the justice dimension was neglected at all. In fact, the potential challenges to validity in the NAGB case may have nothing to do with imbalance per se, at least not initially. From the beginning, the evaluation team appears to have given fair opportunity for all stakeholder voices to be heard, while conducting the evaluation in such a way that the interests of the most vulnerable stakeholders were well represented. Each of the three formative reports was submitted to scrutiny in public forums, allowing adequate opportunity for feedback concerning any difficulties in the clarity or technical quality of the evaluation leading up to those points. In each of these three reports, the evaluation team raised serious concerns about the standard-setting process with no objections, rebuttals, or qualifications from NAGB staff.

But, something important changed between the delivery of those three reports and the delivery of the draft summative report. In Stufflebeam's (2000) recounting, after the third formative report was delivered, NAGB staff asked the evaluation team not to finish the summative report stating that the "assignment was complete" (p. 298). About a month later NAGB staff again contacted Stufflebeam, asking that his team submit a summative evaluation, explaining that "state-level critics had protested that NAGB had not fulfilled the congressional requirement for an external summative evaluation of the achievement levels project" (p. 289) and that the report was needed within the next month. Stufflebeam and his colleagues got to work immediately, even, at the urging of the NAGB, without obtaining a formal contract. The context now shifted from a reasonably paced, contractually binding, formative evaluation, in which information is provided primarily for program staff for the purpose of improvement, to a rushed, contract-free, summative evaluation, in which information is provided primarily for the group to whom program staff are accountable for the purpose of final judgment.

In the rushed shift between contexts, the evaluation team may have overlooked important aspects of both truth and beauty. Despite the apparent technical quality of the evaluation, the team left themselves vulnerable to potentially legitimate criticism on the truth dimension of validity. In science and evaluation, there is more to truth than technical merit.

> *Scientific statements can* never be certain; they can *be only more or less credible.* And *credibility* is a term in individual psychology, i.e., a term that *has meaning only with respect to an individual observer.* To say that some proposition is credible is, after all, to say that it is believed by an agent who is free not to believe it, that is, by an observer who, after exercising judgment and (possibly) intuition, chooses to accept the proposition as worthy of his believing it. (Weizenbaum, 1976 as cited in House, 1980, p. 71, *emphasis ours*)

As House explains, a major component of truth in evaluation is the negotiated agreement on beginning, or foundational, premises. He explains, "The development of an evaluation argument presupposes agreement on the part of the audiences. The premises of the argument are the beginning of this agreement and the point from which larger agreement is built" (1980, p. 76). According to House, agreements "derived from the *negotiation* that often precede the evaluation—*agreements between sponsors, program personnel, and evaluators*" are potentially the most important agreements for a particular evaluation (p. 78, *emphasis ours*). House stresses the importance of this negotiation and notes that elements subject to negotiation, and hence elements for which agreement is crucial, include criteria, methods, and procedures. "Disagreement on these points can destroy the entire credibility of the evaluation (p. 78)." As he summarizes, "the evaluator must start from where his audiences are, even though the beginning premises may not be acceptable to other parties nor to the evaluator himself. Otherwise the evaluation will not be credible or persuasive (pp. 78–79)." If there is no agreement on beginning principles, there is likely to be disagreement about the truth of resulting conclusions. Indeed, as we will emphasize in what follows, establishing not only agreement, but a record of agreement can be critical for resolving potential disagreement about answers to evaluation questions.

Values and Validity in the Context of Evaluation Practice

So, what does it look like when the evaluator appropriately balances these three dimensions in an evaluation? The second evaluator from the MSAP case provides an illustration. She was able to attend to the truth aspect of validity in the design she chose—that is, a quasi-experimental design to answer causal-type evaluation questions. But, by collaboratively developing a logic model that was used to advocate for the need for going beyond the simple "what works" question, in addition to strengthening the truth dimension, she was able to (a) address the justice dimension by including other voices in the evaluation besides the federal funding agency and (b) address the beauty dimension by creating a visual framework that was deemed credible by all stakeholders. This also provides evidence that the weighing of these dimensions can occur at any point in the process, not just in the final synthesis.

Further, as can be garnered from the NAGB case, balancing and negotiating these dimensions must begin at the start of an evaluation and continue throughout. Stufflebeam states that his experience with the NAGB taught him the lesson that it is unwise to work without a contract. We suggest, in harmony with Stufflebeam, establishing a jointly endorsed record of the negotiation is almost as important as the negotiation itself. This is because failing or neglecting to establish explicit, documented agreement on the basic premises and other foundational aspects of the evaluation can result in misunderstandings and differing recollections of the points of agreement. This, in turn, impacts not only the truth dimension of validity, but also the beauty. Different views of the context result in different prescriptions for action and hence different views about the criteria for evaluating the success of any undertaking. It is possible that the NAGB had a different view of the standard-setting process that resulted in disagreement about the deficiencies pointed out by the evaluation team. Perhaps they agreed that there were deficiencies but disagreed about the relative importance of the elements in which deficiencies were found. On such a view, the deficiencies might be seen as something to continue to refine, but of sufficiently minimal importance that the standards produced were both acceptable and the best option available. Or, the NAGB may have agreed both with the assessment of deficiencies and of their importance, but disagreed about what would constitute a solution to the problem. They could have legitimately believed they had addressed the source of the deficiency, and seen the evaluation team's criticisms in the draft summative report as irrelevant to what they had understood to be the problem. Either of these scenarios would present a legitimate disagreement with the team's evaluative conclusions, presenting a challenge to the validity of the evaluative argument.

So, how can an evaluator go about appropriately balancing these dimensions to produce valid evaluations? House provides us with an answer when he says, "the validity of an evaluation depends upon whether the evaluation is true, credible, and normatively correct" (House, 1980, p. 255). Validity requires all three. Striking the right balance requires careful and consistent consideration of each dimension before the evaluation commences, during the evaluation, and even after the evaluation has ended. The evaluator must be careful about giving priority to any one of the three. It is perhaps more productive to use this system as a set of checks and balances. In doing so, one is forced to ask oneself, "What values am I privileging?" "What influence will privileging those values have on the evaluation?" and "How can I attend to these issues in a balanced manner?" Giving more than a little priority to any one dimension may undermine all three. For example, too much priority on social justice is likely to blind the evaluator to some aspects of the truth. Decisions based on the errors are likely to cause harm to someone, potentially even the group the evaluator set out to protect. Too much emphasis on trying to please everyone in terms of acceptable questions and methodology is likely to water down the evaluation and create a sea of potentially conflicting findings in which important evaluative information could get lost. Too little attention to the framing of the evaluation—or stakeholder and evaluator fundamental views of the evidence, the nature and purpose of the evaluation, the criteria, or the relevant evaluation questions—can lead to controversy over the legitimacy of evaluation findings and to little or no use of these findings.

Turning back to a point we made earlier in the chapter, what should an evaluator do when forced to choose between dimensions? As was mentioned earlier, House himself notes that it is not uncommon for an evaluator to intensely focus on one dimension to the exclusion of the other two dimensions. He further argues, "in those concrete instances in which truth and beauty conflict, truth is more important than beauty. And justice more important than either" (p. 117). So for House, when forced to privilege one dimension over the others, and knowing that giving priority to one could undermine the entire process, he chooses justice first, then truth, and last beauty. Thus, he puts fairness and social justice above all else. While we agree with much of House's writings, it is here that we take a departure from him. In our view, abandoning truth for justice risks losing both. Truth must be given priority, but it must be a truth that is both scientifically and culturally humble. This is a truth that takes careful note of the subtle intersection of truth and beauty where they converge around credibility. For something to be credible, it must be both meaningful and coherent to its audience. If one scrupulously attends to this quality of truth, then justice is present in that the evaluation genuinely examines the context from different perspectives, heeding the voices of all relevant stakeholders; it can thus be judged to be normatively correct. We believe that one cannot adequately attend to the truth dimension *without* acknowledging the intersection of truth and beauty around credibility, and thus, also attending to the justice dimension. The dimensions are intertwined and demand appropriate balance. We agree with House that social justice is *truly* of utmost importance, but without *truth* one cannot say so. Of course, without beauty few will understand what is said.

Notes

1. The Magnet Schools Assistance Program (MSAP) is currently authorized under Title V, Part A, of the Elementary and Secondary Act, as amended in 1994 and is administered by the Office of Innovation and Improvement. According to the U.S. Department of Education, the MSAP "provides grants to eligible local educational agencies to establish and operate magnet schools that are operated under a court-ordered or federally approved voluntary desegregation plan" (retrieved from http://www2.ed.gov/programs/magnet/index.html on September 25, 2011). A common identifier of magnet schools is their intended structure around a distinctive educational curriculum or theme (Ballou, 2009). Examples of magnet themes include STEM, language immersion, visual and performing arts, and international baccalaureate.

2. Readers wishing to know more about the NAGB evaluation than is provided here should consult the extensive documentation of this process, and in particular, this evaluation (cf. Stufflebeam, 2000; U.S. General Accounting Office, 1993; Vinovskis, 1998).

References

Ballou, D. (2009). Magnet school outcomes. In M. Berends & M. G. Springer (Eds.), *Handbook of research on school choice* (pp. 409–426). New York, NY: Routledge.

Cizek, G. C. (1993, August). *Reactions to National Academy of Education report, "Setting performance standards for student achievement."* Unpublished manuscript. Retrieved from http://www.eric.ed.gov/contentdelivery/servlet/ERICServlet?accno=ED360397

Campbell, D., & Stanley, J. (1966). *Experimental and quasi-experimental designs for research.* Chicago, IL: Rand McNally.

NEW DIRECTIONS FOR EVALUATION • DOI: 10.1002/ev

Chen, H. T., Donaldson, S. I., & Mark, M. M. (Eds.). (2011). *New Directions for Evaluation: No. 130. Advancing validity in outcome evaluation: Theory and practice.* San Francisco, CA: Jossey-Bass.

Collins, J., Hall, N., & Paul, L. (Eds.). (2004). *Causation and counterfactuals.* Cambridge: MIT Press.

Cook, T. D., & Campbell, D. T. (1979). *Quasi-experimentation: Design and analysis issues for field settings.* Chicago, IL: Rand-McNally.

Cronbach, L. J. (1982). *Designing evaluations of educational and social programs.* San Francisco, CA: Jossey-Bass.

Cronbach, L. J., & Meehl, P. E. (1955). Construct validity in psychological tests. *Psychological Bulletin, 52,* 281–302. doi:10.1037/h0040957

Donaldson, S. I. (2007). *Program theory-driven evaluation science: Strategies and applications.* New York, NY: Routledge.

House, E. R. (1980). *Evaluating with validity.* Beverly Hills, CA: Sage.

Kane, M. (1993, November). *Comments on the NAE evaluation of the NAGB achievement levels.* Unpublished manuscript. Retrieved from http://www.eric.ed.gov/contentdelivery/servlet/ERICServlet?accno=ED360398

Linn, R., Koretz, D., Barker, E., & Burstein, L. (1991). *The validity and credibility of the achievement levels for the 1990 National Assessment of Educational Progress in Mathematics (Center for the Study of Evaluation Report No. 330).* Los Angeles, CA: Center for Research on Evaluation, Standards, and Student Testing, University of California at Los Angeles.

Morgan, S. L. & Winship, C. (2007). *Counterfactuals and causal inference: Methods and principles for social research.* Cambridge, UK: Cambridge University Press.

Murnane, R. J., & Willett, J. B. (2010). *Methods matter: Improving causal inference in educational and social science research.* New York, NY: Oxford University Press.

National Assessment Governing Board (NAGB). (1991, August 14). *Response to the draft summative evaluation report on the National Assessment Governing Board's inaugural effort to set achievement levels on the National Assessment of Educational Progress.* Washington, DC: Author.

Parsons, L. S. (2001, April). *Reducing bias in a propensity score matched-pair sample using Greedy matching techniques.* Paper presented at the Annual SAS Users Group International Conference, Long Beach, CA.

Rubin, D. B. (1997). Estimating causal effects from large data sets using propensity scores. *Annals of Internal Medicine, 127,* 757–763. doi:10.7326/0003-4819-127-8-Part 2-199710151-00064

Scriven, M. (1976). Maximizing the power of causal investigations: The modus operandi method. In G. V. Glass (Ed.), *Evaluation studies review annual* (pp. 101–118). Beverly Hills, CA: Sage.

Scriven, M. (1991). *Evaluation thesaurus* (4th ed.). Newbury Park, CA: Sage.

Shadish, W. R. (2011). The truth about validity. In H. T. Chen, S. I. Donaldson, & M. M. Mark (Eds.), *New Directions for Evaluation: No. 130. Advancing validity in outcome evaluation: Theory and practice* (pp. 107–117). San Francisco, CA: Jossey-Bass. doi:10.1002/ev.369

Shadish, W. R., Cook, T. D., & Campbell, D. T. (2001). *Experimental and quasi-experimental designs for generalized causal inference.* Boston, MA: Houghton Mifflin.

Shepard, L. A., Glaser, R., Linn, R. L., & Bohrnstedt, G. (1993). *Setting performance standards for student achievement* (final report). Stanford, CA: National Academy of Education.

Stufflebeam, D. L. (2000). Lessons in contracting for evaluations. *American Journal of Evaluation, 21,* 293–314. doi:10.1177/109821400002100302

Stufflebeam, D. L., Jaeger, R. M., & Scriven, M. (1991, August). *Summative evaluation of the National Assessment Governing Board's inaugural effort to set achievement levels of the National Assessment of Educational Progress.* Draft report submitted to NAGB on August 1, 1991.

U.S. General Accounting Office. (1993). *Educational achievement standards: NAGB's approach yields misleading interpretations.* Washington, DC: United States General Accounting Office.

Vinovskis, M. (1998). *Overseeing the nation's report card: The creation and evolution of the National Assessment Governing Board (NAGB).* Washington, DC: National Assessment Governing Board.

JAMES C. GRIFFITH is a doctoral candidate for a dual degree in philosophy and psychology at the Claremont Graduation University and a lead evaluator at the Claremont Evaluation Center.

BIANCA MONTROSSE-MOORHEAD is an assistant professor in the Measurement, Evaluation and Assessment program, a research scientist for the Collaborative on Strategic Education Reform (CSER), and coordinator of the Graduate Certificate Program in Program Evaluation at the University of Connecticut.

NEW DIRECTIONS FOR EVALUATION • DOI: 10.1002/ev

Davidson, E. J. (2014). How "beauty" can bring truth and justice to life. In J. C. Griffith & B. Montrosse-Moorhead (Eds.), *Revisiting truth, beauty, and justice: Evaluating with validity in the 21st century. New Directions for Evaluation, 142,* 31–43.

3

How "Beauty" Can Bring Truth and Justice to Life

E. Jane Davidson

Abstract

Quantitative evidence is the "bones," qualitative evidence is the "flesh," and evaluative reasoning is the "vital organs" that bring them both to life. True "beauty" in evaluation is a clearly reasoned, well-crafted, coherent evaluation story that weaves all three of these together to unlock both truth and justice with breathtaking clarity. This chapter provides tips for delivering truly accessible, assumption-unearthing, values-explicit evaluation that clearly lays out: (a) a set of high-level explicitly evaluative questions to frame and focus the work; (b) the justice principles and other values applied in order to answer them; (c) the criteria and evidence that demonstrate performance relative to those principles and values; and (d) the evaluative reasoning used to arrive at robust conclusions about not just what has happened but how good, valuable, and important it is. © Wiley Periodicals, Inc., and the American Evaluation Association.

House, in his 1980 book *Evaluating with Validity*, argued that truth trumps beauty and justice trumps them both. In other words, get the social justice priorities right, deliver valid answers relative to those, and then convey it all beautifully and believably.

I'd like to flip House's idea on its head. What if beauty wasn't merely about how well the evaluative story is told? What if the *process* of creating a clear, compelling, and coherent (beautiful) evaluative story was in fact the key to unlocking validity (truth) and fairness (justice)?

NEW DIRECTIONS FOR EVALUATION, no. 142, Summer 2014 © Wiley Periodicals, Inc., and the American Evaluation Association. Published online in Wiley Online Library (wileyonlinelibrary.com) • DOI: 10.1002/ev.20083

The Importance of Beauty

"Beauty" is about the aesthetics of evaluation—the language, the imagery, the coherence of the story told—and how well it presents a compelling and persuasive argument that is credible to all the various stakeholder audiences. House (1980) describes how the beauty of evaluation lies in how well it tells a story in which the evidence, inferences, and interpretations are integrated into a whole.

In my own evaluation practice, it has become clear to me that well-crafted and coherent form is much more than an aesthetic consideration. It is a critically important route to achieving the clarity and coherence of thinking needed to get the evaluation right.

The "core" of our discipline, the essential piece that makes or breaks evaluation, is evaluative reasoning. Sound, transparent evaluative reasoning produces robust and defensible answers that are not only credible (high "beauty" value) but also valid (high "truth" value, in House's terms). So where does "justice" come in?

Evaluative reasoning is an inherently value-infused task. It is no mere coincidence that the word e-*valu*-ation contains the word "value." Getting the "values" part right is the core of evaluation's validity, and it *includes* getting the justice aspects right.

The justice piece is as much about the "what" as it is about the "who" and the "how" (Davidson, 2010b). More specifically,

- Is everyone who has a *right* to be at the table there, in sufficient numbers, and does the participation protocol and process encourage and enable them to engage meaningfully?
- Are the right voices at the table to correctly and justly determine, for example, what outcomes *should* be considered "valuable" and how much of them would be "enough"?
- Does the evidence gathered adequately capture the realities for those who have historically been marginalized or underserved by the system?
- Have we adequately infused a social justice lens on the findings to highlight inequitable outcomes and other issues, such as barriers to access or participation?

If the people, the process, the evidence, and the reasoning are right, then evaluation has a good chance of not just producing valid and credible findings, but of fulfilling its social justice obligations. By this I mean we become a positive force for change by delivering value-infused, justice-oriented insights in a persuasive form that allows clients to understand what really matters and take action for social betterment (Henry, 2000).

Consensus on what is fair, valuable, and important does not just fall easily out of well-designed evaluation processes. These questions are inherently political, frequently murky, contestable, and often highly contentious. I certainly do not seek to trivialize the challenges of realizing House's aspirations for valid, just, and coherent evaluation in the face of all that swirls around it. What I will do is highlight some of the places where we as evaluators—and the clients who work with us—*avoidably* slip off the rails. I will propose some practically grounded and value-driven strategies to help us get closer to the goal.

A Story of Incoherence

A few years ago, I was asked to review a set of half a dozen program evaluations. The client could not see anything technically wrong with them, but somehow they just weren't delivering what was needed.

As I perused the reports, the first thing that struck me was how few had actually delivered insights or answers into *anything* important, let alone with clarity. What had gone wrong?

Conspicuously missing from a large proportion of the reports was any set of guiding questions up front to give a clear sense of what we were trying to find out. Many just leapt immediately into measurement or qualitative exploration of the programs and their outcomes. By the end of these reports, I was still none the wiser about whether the entire program had in fact been a waste of time, effort, and money. It was not clear which were the most crucially important findings, let alone their implications for policy, programming, or practice.

Some of the evaluations had questions upfront, but unfortunately they were too narrow to be of much use. Typical were questions asking how much "indicator X" had changed. Where was the qualitative "flesh" on these quantitative "bones" to tell us what had *really* changed in people's lives? Where were the "vital organs," the evaluative elements, the parts that told us whether the outcome was good enough, worthwhile, important, life-changing, or barely worth the effort put into achieving it?

I was more hopeful when I saw that some of the reports had asked quite good high-level questions at the front end. Some of the questions were even evaluative in nature, that is, they asked not just what the results were, but whether they were any good. Unfortunately, what followed was anything but actual answers. A more accurate characterization would be "free association" to the questions using any data that seemed relevant.

These "Rorschach inkblot evaluations" (Davidson, 2010a) completely failed to deliver coherent answers to the questions that had—promisingly—been posed at the front end. As such, the reports had low "truth value," but not usually because the "ingredients" of truth were missing. There was often enough evidence contained in the report where satisfactory answers *could* have been produced. The problem was that they *weren't*.

Put simply, the lack of "beauty" (a clear, compelling, and persuasive evaluative argument) was *an important reason why* we ended up with a lack of "truth" (no valid answers to important high-level questions). It was not that valid answers had been formulated but not conveyed clearly.

Where was the "beauty" lacking, and how did that keep us from getting to "truth"? In these cases, the key elements were:

- *Questions*: A lack of high-level explicitly evaluative questions to frame and focus the work.
- *Answers*: Where there were questions, the so-called "answers" were free association using any relevant data rather than direct and reasoned responses to the questions posed.
- *Synthesis*: Where there were multiple sources of evidence pertaining to a particular issue, there was no attempt to synthesize or weave the evidence together.
- *Evaluative conclusions*: The evaluative reasoning piece was missing, so we never got a clear sense of whether the results were any good or not.

How could evaluation contractors miss something as fundamental as the need to actually deliver answers to important client questions? And how could clients miss the importance of insisting on actual answers? It's a bit like rocket science—the theory is simple (forces up = forces down; just answer some important questions); it's the execution that's a challenge.

Why Are Some Evaluations So "Incoherent"?

One of the roots of our incoherence lies, I believe, in where many of us hail from in our formal education and training. Social science teaches us how to break down our evaluation (or research) questions into criteria, indicators, and sources of evidence. But it does not tell us how to integrate them, how to weave evidence, or how to tell a compelling story in answer to important evaluation questions (Davidson, 2007; House, 1980).

Many so-called "mixed methods" evaluations are in fact nothing more than "both methods." They present qualitative and quantitative evidence separately, with no attempt to synthesize and make sense of complementary or even contradictory stories that emerge from the different perspectives and data sources.

There is something else that is needed too, something that training in the social sciences does not equip us with. It is the explicitly evaluative piece, what Scriven (2003) calls *The Something More List*. Not many of us have been lucky enough to add this rich repertoire to our toolkits. And, as my next vignette illustrates, it is a grave mistake to underestimate how hard it is for even well-trained researchers to grasp and use evaluative reasoning and evaluation-specific methodology. Quantitative evidence is the "bones," qualitative evidence the "flesh," and evaluative reasoning the "vital organs" that bring them both to life. If we are missing any of these we simply cannot craft a coherent evaluative story.

NEW DIRECTIONS FOR EVALUATION • DOI: 10.1002/ev

The Story of the Evaluation (Not)

A few years ago, I agreed to collaborate with a firm of applied researchers and consultants to work in an advisory role on an evaluation of a social program. We spent significant time at the front end framing the high-level evaluation questions, and the client was pleased with what it looked like they would get from the evaluation.

When the first draft of the report came through, I was dismayed to see that the researchers had completely missed a critically important aspect of what we were doing that seemed blindingly obvious to me. The whole point of framing the evaluation around high-level questions in the first place was that we would actually answer them.

As one might expect from highly competent applied researchers, the data collection instruments and the evidence collected were fine. For almost all of our high-level evaluation questions, we had a strong range of evidence to draw from—insights from participants and supervisors, both quantitative (survey data) and qualitative (interviews), plus our own direct observations and document reviews.

The real issue lay in the coherence of how it was woven together—particularly the evaluative reasoning. Instead of considering the evidence as a set and weaving it together to create a compelling answer to that question, the evidence was laid out in separate sections (surveys and then interviews) and never synthesized, let alone interpreted evaluatively to say how good the results were.

I provided extensive feedback on the first draft and showed how we needed to reframe and reorder the report so we could craft coherently reasoned, well-evidenced answers to the questions we had posed. It wouldn't be a quick task to do this, but it was perfectly doable because all the ingredients were there.

When the second draft came through, the reframing had not been done at all, and only minor tweaks incorporated. The project manager explained that it would have been too time consuming (they had run out of budgeted time), and in any case his staff members who were writing the report would have needed very extensive guidance to show them what needed to be done. At this point, I felt that what we had promised the client and what we had ended up delivering were so vastly different—and at odds with my own advice—that I asked for my name to be removed from the report.

What the client most needed was a set of coherent answers to the important questions that had been agreed upon at the outset. Like the earlier-mentioned reports I reviewed, we had all the right ingredients—the right mix of evidence and the opportunity to make well-reasoned sense of it—but the unwoven and evaluative reasoning-free approach to presenting the evidence meant that we delivered a nonanswer. It wasn't that we *had* valid answers and had just failed to *convey* them in a coherent report (i.e., truth without beauty). The fact that we didn't clearly lay out the evaluation

New Directions for Evaluation • DOI: 10.1002/ev

questions and then systematically synthesize the evidence using evaluative reasoning meant that we never arrived at an answer at all (i.e., no beauty →no truth).

Even if the relevant evidence pertaining to each question had been integrated in some way, it was a fatal problem that the applied researchers' toolkit lacked the one crucial tool needed to do that—*evaluation-specific methodology* (Davidson, 2005; Scriven, 1991, 2003; Scriven & Davidson, 2013). These are the tools, methods, and underlying logic that are specific to evaluation, not just borrowed from elsewhere.

I recently listed some examples of evaluation-specific methodologies (Davidson, 2013b), which include

- needs and values assessment;
- merit determination methodologies (blending values with evidence about performance, e.g., with evaluative rubrics);
- importance weighting methodologies (both qualitative and quantitative);
- evaluative synthesis methodologies (combining evaluative ratings on multiple dimensions or components to come to overall conclusions); and
- value-for-money analysis (not just standard cost-effective analysis or social return on investment, but also options that can deal with intangibles as well as financial considerations).

In contrast, the following would *not* count as evaluation-specific: statistics; experimental or quasi-experimental designs; any of the standard research methods (interviews, focus groups, observation, surveys, content analysis, etc.); or even the multitude of methods for inferring causation (BetterEvaluation, 2013b; Davidson, 2013a).

What did I learn from this experience? Three lessons:

- The "core" of our discipline—the evaluation-specific "values" part—is often the most important; it makes or breaks validity of evaluation time and again.
- "Token" evaluation expertise on the team is not enough.
- Never assume even experienced researchers can quickly pick up the skills needed to do evaluation!

Sound Evaluative Reasoning—What It Looks Like

House's (1980, Chapter 1 in this issue) conceptualization of "truth" has at its center the notion of well-reasoned evaluative argument. What, exactly, constitutes a sound evaluative argument? I have written about this elsewhere in the context of the practical, values-explicit Actionable Evaluation framework (Davidson, 2012, 2013b). Actionable Evaluation provides a set of concepts, principles, and practical guidelines for asking the most important questions and delivering straight-to-the-point answers and insights that can be used to inform thinking and/or action. Its six key elements are:

1. clear purpose,
2. right engagement,
3. important questions,
4. reasoned answers,
5. succinct reporting, and
6. actionable insights.

Actionable Evaluation can help us better deliver on evaluation that is strong on both truth and justice largely through its attention to beauty—clarity, coherence, and simplicity. First, the overall framing, the structure, and the process help ensure that the right people are at the evaluative table for the right reasons and that the values are explicitly and justly dealt with and not merely glossed over. In addition, the last two steps—succinct reporting and actionable insights—pay sharp attention to the kind of clarity and coherence that fosters reflection, insight, engagement, and use.

Step 4, reasoned answers, is (in my view) the "core" of what House is referring to when he mentions well-reasoned evaluative argument. And step 5, succinct reporting, is central to presenting the argument coherently. These are the steps I will focus on here. Readers who wish to know more about the other steps are referred to the minibook itself.

Reasoned Answers That Are Clear, Direct, and Explicitly Evaluative

This is essentially the methodological "core" of evaluation logic and methodology that defines our discipline. The absolutely fundamental difference between evaluation and other related activities, such as research, monitoring, performance measurement, and audit is that we ask and answer explicitly evaluative questions (i.e., questions about quality, value, and importance; see also Davidson, 2013b).

The basic steps to evaluative reasoning are listed below. Note that steps 1, 2, and 3 are where justice considerations are explicitly factored in:

1. For each of the high-level evaluation questions, list all the relevant criteria of merit—these are the *aspects* of something that are potentially "good"/"bad"/"just"/"unjust"/"valuable"/"detrimental" about it.
2. Determine the relative importance of the criteria—some are more important than others (e.g., outcomes for those with the most serious needs); some are nice to have but not that important.
3. Define "how good is good," that is, what the "constellation of evidence" on each criterion would look like in order to say something was "good," "barely acceptable," "unacceptable," or "excellent," for example—including whether there is some minimum level of

performance that should be considered acceptable (e.g., adequate accessibility for vulnerable populations, as a justice consideration).

4. Gather and analyze the right mix of evidence, being sure to triangulate using multiple sources.
5. Draw evaluative conclusions about performance on each of the criteria by interpreting the evidence (4) against the definitions of "how good is good" (3).
6. Synthesize these subevaluations (performances on several criteria) to draw overall evaluative conclusions about the program/policy/etc. as a whole.

Figure 3.1. Evaluative Interpretation Funnel

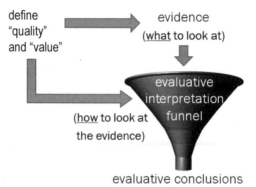

Source: From Davidson (2012). Reprinted with permission.

I often use the "evaluative interpretation funnel" depicted in Figure 3.1 as another way of explaining this logic. Fundamentally, we begin by defining "quality" and "value" (using a justice lens). We do this in two ways. One is identifying the criteria (and thereby the evidence), we will examine to work out whether something is "good" or not (step 1). The other—and often-skipped—task is to say *how* we will look at the evidence, that is, how we define "how good is good" on each criterion (step 3).

Working out how to look at the evidence (step 3) is constructing the evaluative interpretation "funnel," which can take many forms. Evaluative rubrics are a particularly useful example because they allow consideration of multiple forms and sources of triangulated evidence at once (Davidson, 2005, 2012). It is by gathering the right evidence (step 4) and passing it through that funnel that we can interpret evaluatively and draw real evaluative conclusions (step 5). These are conclusions that say not just *what* the findings were, but *how good or worthwhile* they were.

These conclusions about performance on each dimension— "subevaluations," as Scriven (2013) calls them—need to be combined to come to an overall answer to each high-level evaluation question.

In addition, there is one further synthesis step to arrive at an overall determination of policy or program merit or worth. To synthesize the subevaluations (step 6), we need the determinations of importance (step 2) and synthesis methodology (BetterEvaluation, 2013a; Davidson, 2005; Scriven, 1994).

Step 5 of the Actionable Evaluation Framework: Succinct Reporting

This is the step where the "beauty" of the evaluation—how straightforward, succinct, intelligible, and coherent it is—becomes a powerful vehicle for crafting (not just conveying) evaluative reasoning that is strong on both truth and justice.

When I reflect on what has improved the quality of my own work in recent years, it has been a relentless push toward succinctness and crystal clarity while grappling with some quite complex and difficult material. For me this means striving to produce simple, direct, and clear answers to evaluative questions and being utterly transparent in the reasoning I have used to get to those conclusions.

Getting there has been a multidecade struggle to "unlearn" the dense, long-winded, academic writing style I inevitably picked up through my formal studies in the social sciences. Such writing is not only difficult and confusing for most people to read; in many cases it is symptomatic of a deeper underlying problem—the thinking behind it is often confused and ill-reasoned.

Research and evaluation reports are not just impenetrable because of the writing; the same can be true of the methods and approaches that are used to conduct research and evaluation in the first place. The American Psychological Association's Task Force on Statistical Inference noted the tendency for researchers to choose sophisticated and complicated analytic methods to impress other academics rather than more elegant, simpler approaches that would be more appropriate and the findings easier to communicate (Wilkinson & The Task Force on Statistical Inference, 1999).

Similarly, Peterson and Park (2010) have lamented how current academic culture erroneously equates methodological complexity with research significance, whereas the evidence suggests the reverse has been the case historically:

> [T]he evidence of history is clear that the research studies with the greatest impact in psychology are *breathtakingly simple* in terms of the questions posed, the methods and designs used, the statistics brought to bear on the data, and the take-home messages. (p. 398, emphasis added)

How often do we see the use of overly complicated and sophisticated evaluation designs and analyses that, although they might unearth some academically interesting nuances, actually render the findings uncommu-nicable to the audiences that use them? Often, in my experience.

Although sophisticated analyses and big words may be beneficial for exhibiting methodological, statistical, and verbal prowess for academics, the major drawback is that they absolutely kill the potential to influence. Communications and data visualization experts have known for years that simple, elegant, clear communication is far more likely influence both thinking and action (Evergreen, 2013; Hayes & Grossman, 2006; Heath & Heath, 2008; Morris, Fitz-Gibbon, & Freeman, 1987).

There's a delicate balance to be struck here between digging deeply enough to do justice to the true complexity of the questions versus getting only a surface grasp of what's really going on. Peterson and Park (2010) go on to say that:

> Simple does not mean simplistic. Nor does it mean easy or quick. Rather, simple means elegant, clear and accessible, not just to other researchers but to the general public. No one's eyes glaze over when hearing about a high-impact study. No one feels stupid. No one asks, "And your point is?" (p. 398)

Beauty, Power, and Justice

Impenetrable language—along with poorly explained and overly compli-cated analysis techniques—have the effect of discouraging engagement and criticism, often to the detriment of those whose voices most need to be heard. "The more technical and quantitative the evaluation the less a naive audience will be able to challenge it" (House, 1980, p. 74). Once again, beauty can kill justice just as easily as it can assassinate truth. I would add an additional issue here about impenetrability.

The "values" that form the core of evaluation—and that need to be ap-plied effectively in order to meet the justice criterion—are not made explicit at all in most evaluations. One can't help but ask whether a not-so-subtle purpose of such evaluations is to *deliberately* make the values, assump-tions, and evaluative reasoning impenetrable, undiscussable, and unable to be criticized.

In my view, the evaluation profession needs to strive to make evalu-ations themselves easier to critique—unpacking the values, assumptions, and evaluative logic so that it's easier for people to see what we've done and to challenge us on any part of it. And, to invite questioning of the broad jus-tice principles that have been applied. Sure, it's riskier in that it opens the evaluation up to criticism, but hey, that's what makes evaluation interesting.

Truth, Beauty, and Justice—Three Decades On

Let's come back to House's original conceptualizations of truth, beauty, and justice: "Truth is the attainment of arguments soundly made, beauty the attainment of coherence well wrought, and justice the attainment of politics fairly done" (House, Chapter 1 in this issue, p. 9).

House also presents some newer challenges to reflect the shifts in context 30 years on:

1. *Truth* cannot be assured on grounds of technical adequacy alone; increasingly important is keeping an eye on conflict of interest and bias, as well as the core element, the validity of the evaluative argument.
2. Our conceptions of *justice* have shifted in the past few decades, with increased emphasis on the perspectives of participants and other impactees, especially women, people of color, and vulnerable populations (e.g., those who are ill, living with disabilities, homeless, and/or living in poverty or conflict zones).
3. On *beauty*: How we frame evaluation is critically important to ensuring we interpret events coherently and meaningfully; when the framing is wrong it can lead to cognitive bias. Care is also needed with the right use of language, voice, imagery, metaphor, and perspective to convey the findings in ways that are appropriate and not misleading.

Again, flipping around the order of House's list, it seems to me that one of the critical spots where evaluation can slip off the rails is in the framing. All too often I see evaluations using a supposedly value-neutral frame, approaching the task as though it is merely a technical or measurement exercise. Evaluations that are pitched as value-neutral are almost invariably (a) Eurocentric and (b) skewed toward the easily measurable—but not necessarily most important—criteria valued by those who already hold positions of privilege and power (and, usually, the budgetary purse strings). When this happens, justice gets short shrift.

Conclusions

Getting the "beauty" part of evaluation right is delivering a truly accessible, assumption-unearthing, values-explicit evaluation that clearly lays out what the big-picture evaluation questions are, what justice principles have been applied in order to answer them, what criteria and evidence have been selected as going straight to the heart of the truth, and how the evaluative inferences have been made to get to the conclusions.

If we get the "beauty" part right, then the all-important "justice" part is more likely to hit the mark—because if it doesn't, that will be easier for critics to identify and criticize.

If the "justice" part is right, the identification of criteria and evidence is less likely to go awry, and the evaluative inferences used to weave the overall story will be more explicit and therefore better. In other words, the "truth" aspect of the evaluation will be stronger.

New Directions for Evaluation • DOI: 10.1002/ev

"Beauty" is not just about making evaluation pretty and palatable; beauty is the clarity of thinking that is essential for getting both the justice/values and truth/validity aspects right.

References

BetterEvaluation. (2013a). *Synthesize*. Retrieved from http://betterevaluation. org/plan/synthesize_value

BetterEvaluation (2013b). *Understand causes*. Retrieved from http://betterevaluation. org/plan/understandcauses

Davidson, E. J. (2005). *Evaluation methodology basics: The nuts and bolts of sound evaluation*. Thousand Oaks, CA: Sage.

Davidson, E. J. (2007). Unlearning some of our social scientist habits. *Journal of Multidisciplinary Evaluation, 4*, iii–vi.

Davidson, E. J. (2010a, November). *Extreme genuine evaluation makeovers (XGEMs)*. Keynote presented at the meeting of the Australasian Evaluation Society, Wellington, New Zealand.

Davidson, E. J. (2010b). "Process values" and "deep values" in evaluation. *Journal of Multidisciplinary Evaluation, 6*, 206–208.

Davidson, E. J. (2012). *Actionable evaluation: Getting succinct answers to the most important questions [minibook]*. New Zealand: Real Evaluation.

Davidson, E. J. (2013a, June). *Causal inference for qualitative and mixed methods*. Workshop presented at the Canadian Evaluation Society Conference, Toronto, Canada.

Davidson, E. J. (2013b). *Monitoring and evaluation: Let's get crystal clear on the difference*. Retrieved from http://genuineevaluation.com/monitoring-and-evaluation -lets-get-crystal-clear-on-the-difference/

Evergreen, S. D. H. (2013). *Presenting data effectively: Communicating your findings for maximum impact*. Thousand Oaks, CA: Sage.

Hayes, R., & Grossman, D. (2006). *A scientist's guide to talking with the media*. Piscataway, NJ: Rutgers University Press.

Heath, C., & Heath, D. (2008). *Made to stick: Why some ideas take hold and others become unstuck* [Kindle edition]. Retrieved from http://www.amazon.com/ Made-Stick-Ideas-Survive-Others-ebook/dp/B000N2HCKQ/ref=tmm_kin_swatch_0? _encoding=UTF8&sr=&qid=

Henry, G. T. (2000). Why not use? In V. J. Caracelli & H. Preskill (Eds.), *New Directions for Evaluation: No. 88. The expanding scope of evaluation use* (pp. 85–98). San Francisco, CA: Jossey-Bass. doi:10.1002/ev.1193

House, E. R. (1980). *Evaluating with validity*. Beverly Hills, CA: Sage. Reissued by Information Age Publications, NC, 2008.

Morris, L. L., Fitz-Gibbon, C. T., & Freeman, M. E. (1987). *How to communicate evaluation findings*. Thousand Oaks, CA: Sage.

Peterson, C., & Park, N. (2010). Keeping it simple. *The Psychologist, 23*, 398–400.

Scriven, M. (1991). *Evaluation thesaurus* (4th ed.). Thousand Oaks, CA: Sage.

Scriven, M. (1994). The final synthesis. *American Journal of Evaluation, 15*, 367–382. doi:10.1177/109821409401500317

Scriven, M. (2003). Evaluation in the new millennium: A transdisciplinary vision. In S. I. Donaldson & M. Scriven (Eds.), *Evaluating social programs and problems* (pp. 19–41). Mahwah, NJ: Erlbaum.

Scriven, M. (2013). *Key evaluation checklist*. Retrieved from http://michaelscriven. info/images/KEC_7.25.2013.pdf

Scriven, M., & Davidson, E. J. (2013, October). *Evaluation-specific methodology.* Workshop facilitated at the American Evaluation Association Conference, Washington, DC.

Wilkinson, L., & The Task Force on Statistical Inference. (1999). Statistical methods in psychology journals: Guidelines and explanations. *American Psychologist, 54,* 594–604.

E. Jane Davidson is the owner and director of Real Evaluation, Ltd.

New Directions for Evaluation • DOI: 10.1002/ev

Hurteau, M., & Williams, D. D. (2014). Credible judgment: Combining truth, beauty, and justice. In J. C. Griffith & B. Montrosse-Moorhead (Eds.), *Revisiting truth, beauty, and justice: Evaluating with validity in the 21st century. New Directions for Evaluation, 142,* 45–56.

4

Credible Judgment: Combining Truth, Beauty, and Justice

Marthe Hurteau, David D. Williams

Abstract

The research summarized in this chapter provides descriptive evidence to support House's vision of validity by expanding connections with his theory to a wide variety of professions, in addition to professional evaluators. Perhaps these results and discussion of them and the emerging model will invite professionals to reflect upon ways to improve their own evaluative judgments. Case study interviews were conducted in Canada and the United States with 27 professionals from many helping professions, including law and law enforcement, social work, medicine, education, business, sports, and chaplaincy. Participants were asked to discuss examples of successful and less successful evaluative judgments they had made in their professional work. Citing patterns discovered through analysis of these contrasting examples, we linked their experiences to House's framework regarding truth, beauty, and justice as foundations for validity. This research thus generated a descriptive model of a process to produce credible evaluation judgments with six interacting elements: (1) credible judgments evolve through an iterative process; (2) frameworks, protocols, and methods may help professionals generate valid evidence, but they are often not sufficient; (3) stakeholders' involvement is essential, and how they participate varies depending on the circumstances; (4) the path required to generate a credible judgment is rarely linear; (5) credible judgment is based on strong argumentation that is properly developed and aesthetically presented; (6) the production of credible judgments

NEW DIRECTIONS FOR EVALUATION, no. 142, Summer 2014 © Wiley Periodicals, Inc., and the American Evaluation Association. Published online in Wiley Online Library (wileyonlinelibrary.com) • DOI: 10.1002/ev.20084

depends on special dispositions, orientations, or qualities of the professionals. © Wiley Periodicals, Inc., and the American Evaluation Association.

Introduction

Evaluating a social or educational program or policy is a practical matter that involves judgment (Cousins & Shulha, 2008; Fitzpatrick, Christie, & Mark, 2009; House & Howe, 1999; Schwandt, 2002; Scriven, 1980). To be useful, this judgment should be credible, which, according to Patton (1997), " ... includes the perceived accuracy, fairness, and believability of it" (p.250). However, Guba (1972), in *The Failure of Educational Evaluation*, pointed out that early on, evaluation judgments were not systematically supported by credible evidence. Various theorists and professional evaluators agree that this concern has continued (Hurteau, Houle, & Mongiat, 2009; Hurteau, Valois & Boissiroy, 2010; Scriven, 1995; Treasury Board of Canada Secretariat, 2004). Undeniably, this weakness constitutes an Achilles heel for the recognition of evaluation as a discipline.

These observations led Hurteau et al. (2012) to conduct research in Canada aimed at developing a model that could describe and provide a better understanding of a process to generate credible evaluation judgments. They published a theoretical model based on 19 cases. Subsequently, eight additional cases were studied in the United States to explore how professionals from a slightly different culture generate evaluation judgments in light of the Canadian claims. Results from both studies are combined briefly as a basis for discussing House's (1980) work on truth, justice, and beauty in evaluation, particularly as these qualities relate to evaluation judgment validity. We recognize that a broad literature on forming credible evidence exists (e.g., Donaldson, Christie & Mark, 2009). For reasons of space and focus, we have chosen not to situate our results within that literature.

Presenting Our Research on Evaluative Judgment

Hurteau et al. (2012) wanted to explore new ways to understand the phenomenon (Schreiber, 2001) of generating a credible judgment. They opted to use grounded methodological framework theory (Strauss & Corbin, 1998), which involves an inductive analysis process that also takes into consideration hypotheses and intuitions that are tested in the field of practice (Gilgun, 2001; Strauss & Corbin, 1998).

Sampling

Agreeing with Stake's (2011) claim that judgment is not only done by professional evaluators, Hurteau et al. (2012) assumed that professionals in many fields (e.g., law, medicine, education, journalism, business, regulatory agencies, intelligence, and military) make evaluative judgments and strive to make them credible to stakeholders judging their evaluation proficiency. Therefore, they used purposive sampling to gather data from a wide variety of professionals in documenting and understanding the phenomenon of making credible evaluation judgments through professional experience.

The initial population consisted of Canadian professionals (with more than five years of practice) in various fields, who all had in common that they make evaluative judgments regularly. A first sample consisted of four professionals (an investigator, a judge, a manager, and a physician). Hypotheses and an initial version of a model based on grounded theory emerged while studying these four cases. Over time, the Canadian researchers sampled 15 other professionals from various backgrounds (two managers, one criminal investigator, one nurse, two police officers, two teachers, one coach, one firefighter, three special educators, one judge, and one lawyer) to participate in additional case studies. They applied the constant comparison analysis procedures of grounded theory building until theoretical saturation was reached through analysis of these 19 cases. The most important criterion for including additional cases was *emergent-fit*, or searching for consistency in all the evidence from the case analyses until new data did not contribute anything new to the emerging model.

In addition, to test further the model's relevance and transferability (Lincoln & Guba, 1985) outside of Canada, eight experienced professionals (two social workers, a chaplain, a detective/sheriff, a paramedic/firefighter, an elementary school teacher, a chiropractor, and a judge) in the United States were studied too.

Data Collection: Methods and Procedure

Hurteau et al. (2012) chose to combine protocol analysis and judgment analysis. These methods are used in judgment and decision making studies. Their pitfalls can be controlled by combining them (Einhorn, Kleinmuntz, & Kleinmuntz, 1979). In particular, protocol analysis relies on verbal descriptions of how people reason and consists of asking individuals to "think aloud" while they work through a series of judgments (Ericsson & Simon, 1993; Kleinmuntz, 1968). In contrast, judgment analysis requires the person to do what they do naturally while an observer develops a model describing the process that produces the judgment (Brehmer & Joyce, 1988; Cooksey, 1996; Hammond, Stewart, Brehmer, & Steinman, 1975).

After obtaining signed consent, the researchers audio-recorded indepth conversational or open question dialogue interviews with each participant. Lasting from 90 to 120 min, interviews started with researchers asking each participant about their understanding of judgment and credibility. Then participants were asked to relate two of their own personal professional experiences, one they considered to have generated a "good" judgment and a second experience that yielded a judgment of lower quality. They were asked to describe the two situations, exploring the processes they used (judgment analysis). Finally, they were asked to "think aloud" to compare the two situations (what was similar and what was different) and to speculate on what they thought could explain the different results (protocol analysis).

Data Analysis

After transcribing the Canadian interviews, a team of five researchers (Hurteau et al., 2012) from various backgrounds analyzed the data. Open coding allowed the researchers to focus on the words and concepts of the participants and to group them into categories (e.g., types of situations, types of contingencies, contexts). They used axial coding to put the categories together, to focus attention on certain elements and distinctions (e.g., between authenticity or the truth of a story and the associated credibility of the participants' judgment), as well as to generate a first draft of a descriptive model. Selective coding allowed the researchers to refine their understanding of "how" and "why" issues as they refined the model to integrate all the categories.

The same interview protocol was used with the sample in the United States, but the analysis focused on testing how well the results from the Hurteau et al. (2012) study emerged from and resonated with the U.S. data. Two researchers read through the transcripts, focusing on data that supported or contrasted with the Canadian codes (Guba & Lincoln, 1989). When negative cases appeared, the elements were modified to reflect those data.

The researchers recognized that any "research product is one rendering among multiple interpretations of a shared reality" (Charmaz, 2002, p.523) and that their own knowledge and experience in evaluation would influence their interpretations of what they learned to an unknown extent. Therefore, other researchers could arrive at different interpretations given their biases, experiences, and so forth. In order to enhance credibility of results and build a strong argument, the researchers followed standards discussed by Lincoln and Guba (1985), including peer review by methodology experts, triangulation, member checks, and negative case analyses.

Results

The emerging model of the credible judgment process used by the professionals in these cases includes several components and simultaneous iterative operations that can be summarized in terms of these six interacting elements:

1. Credible judgments evolve through an iterative process.
2. Frameworks, protocols, and methods may help professionals generate valid evidence, but they are often not sufficient.

3. Stakeholders' involvement is essential, and how they participate varies depending on the circumstances.
4. The path required to generate a credible judgment is rarely linear.
5. Credible judgment is based on strong argumentation that is properly developed and aesthetically presented.
6. The production of credible judgments depends on special dispositions, orientations, or qualities of the professionals.

After presenting an overview of House's (1980) work, the following discussion will explore these six interacting elements and examine how each one relates to House's work.

Linking the Research Results With House's Views on Validity

House (2010) explained that reflection upon his practice led him to develop his concept of evaluation validity in terms of truth, beauty, and justice. Through reflective analysis of 27 case studies, we provide evidence that supports his original vision as articulated in his own works.

First, House claims that valid "evaluations are the best judgments we can arrive at in the situation" (House, 1995, p. 38). He elaborates that in order to be considered valid, an evaluation must be true, coherent (beautiful), and just. The criteria support a prescriptive perspective. However, he clarifies that truth is "an ideal which can only be approximated through an interplay of introspection and public verification" (House, 1980, p. 88). Evaluation is a search for an understanding or judgment, supported by arguments that are believable or credible to concerned audiences.

Second, "beauty" refers to aesthetic qualities, such as coherence and appropriate forms of communication that support credibility of an evaluation argument. As House (1980) states, " the evaluation must be credible so that the audience finds it trustworthy" (p. 255) and "the story itself can be more or less tightly integrated, and it provides the necessary coherence for the evaluation as a whole" (House, 1979, p. 9). Also, "people often judge the credibility of reported events on the basis of aesthetic criteria like vividness and inherent unity . . . ; aesthetic form transforms the content into a new, self-contained whole" (p. 14).

Third, House (1980) claims "evaluation should not only be true; it should also be just" (p. 121). More precisely, "conceptions of justice act more as broad frameworks of considerations rather that as internally consistent machines for deducing conclusions. They distribute the burdens of argument in particular ways" (p. 120).

Finally, these three concepts are required to generate credible evaluation judgments and they are combined and contextualized in House's

(1980) view, as stated in this summary, " truth is more important than beauty. And justice more important that either" (p. 117).

Linking These Views With Research Results

In the following section, each element identified through analysis of 27 cases is clarified, statements from the case studies are quoted, and connections to House's work are suggested, although only a few illustrative quotes are shared due to space constraints. The researchers found that all the cases and House's work provided solid evidence to support all the elements, and other publications are being prepared to share the thick descriptions of the professionals' statements about their evaluation judgment making. Negative case analyses did not present strong evidence contrary to these elements, but slight modifications to them, which led to the presentation shared here.

1. *Credible judgments come through an iterative process.* Interviewees' experiences clarified that judgment evolves, as evidence unfolds and is analyzed and arguments credible to audiences emerge. For example, a detective shared his thinking about how a young first time offender would react to different decisions the legal system could make, discussed options with others, and finally made a choice to not "throw the book" at the offender but found a way for him to make restitution and move forward with his life, outside the court and jail system. The credibility of this evaluation became clearer over years, as he and other stakeholders saw this boy doing well in school. House (1980) supported this element by stating that "the evaluator must build [evaluation judgments] upon agreements with the audiences" (p. 78).

2. *Frameworks, methods, and protocols may help professionals generate valid evidence, but they are often not sufficient to make judgments credible to stakeholders.* Interviewees acknowledged that even though rules and evidence are essential to generating valid evidence and analyzing it, they are insufficient alone to produce credible judgments stakeholders will accept. As a nurse stated,

> The protocol is 8 hrs. But, I could not wait 8 hours. It was obvious that she had a distended bladder. I could not leave her like this. I didn't even call the doctor. It is my professional judgment that said, no, I do not wait 8 hours. I installed the catheter immediately, and called the doctor later on. He told me that it was okay.

House (1979) supports this view,

> Credibility of the evaluation depends partly on the correspondence of the quantitative part to the principles of measurement, the correspondence of the qualitative part to the personal experience of the audience, and the

correspondence of the parts to one another. If all these elements fit together properly, and the evaluation was aesthetically rendered, then the entire evaluation would be seen as highly credible. (p. 13)

Chelimsky (2006), Chen (2005), and Schwandt (2009) also support the view. Indeed, "however necessary, developing credible evidence in evaluation is not sufficient for establishing the credibility of an evaluation" (Schwandt, 2009, p. 209).

3. *Stakeholders' involvement is essential and how they participate varies depending on the circumstances* Audiences assume active roles in interpreting judgments through ongoing dialogue and serious discourse. As a special educator noted, "there's a team behind every good judgment." Another special educator said, "For me, the judgment emerges through the confrontation with others. I'm not saying that I cannot emit a judgment. I'm just saying that if we want to enrich our professional judgment, we have to confront it with others." House (1980) supported this view when he said, "Truth is an ideal which can only be approximated through interplay of introspection and public verification" (p.88). For Smith (2011), although evaluators' and stakeholders' roles and responsibilities are hard to identify, it is clear that both have important roles in forming judgments.

4. *The path required to generate a credible judgment is rarely linear.* All interviewees shared this view, but particularly the schoolteacher, chaplain, investigator, chiropractor, nurse, social workers, special educator, firefighters, police, and judges. Like a special educator mentioned: "You start the evaluation by putting things in place and continue as you progress, because people will always give you new elements. Your evaluation never finishes. Tomorrow it is another thing. We put it all together to get an idea of where we are." The interviewees described the need for flexible use of many types of information from different sources at all and repeating stages, leading them to explore new paths, requiring them to revisit and revise various choices. As a social worker noted about a poor judgment she and her colleagues made in which they used a process that was too linear:

[Following my boss' direction], I called his caseworker, who supervised services for disabilities, to let him know we would be taking him off services. And that was all that I did. When he was off of our services, still home, not getting any help, he had a medical emergency and had to go back to the ER. It would have been better if we had talked to Adult Protective Services to tell them that he wasn't safe [or] able to make that decision to stay at home. [Looking back], we should have just stayed in there and provided the care, even though it was an iffy situation.

Though we could not find evidence that House addressed this element in his original work, we learned in sharing our conclusions with him during an American Evaluation Association annual meeting session that he supports our and Smith's (2011) claims that credible judgments emerge from a nonlinear process that constantly adapts to newly available information. The standards of justice and beauty are exemplified in this flexible process, which is sensitive to changing contexts, needs, and interests of clients.

5. *Credible judgment is based on strong argumentation that is properly developed and aesthetically presented.* Arguments consist of reasons that connect goals, evidence, and emerging judgment. A manager noted, "All points of view must be present in the judgment. Arguments must point out why some facts are withheld and others not. It's a reflective/evaluative process, and all the information is linked together." However, in addition to a strong argument (content), the way it is presented (format) is also vital. As a judge noted, "Judgment is above all an act of communication. It must include all points of view and be accessible." House (1980) supports this perspective by offering his "logic of evaluative argument" to address the "truth" criterion. And, in his chapter on beauty, he claims that evaluators must find ways to present and support their judgments so audiences can readily receive them: "People often judge the credibility of reported events on the basis of aesthetic criteria like vividness and inherent unity—on appearances" (p.113). Likewise, the evaluator "must address issues and construct arguments that appeal to particular audiences" (House, 1980, p. 75).

6. *The production of credible judgments engages special dispositions of the professionals.* Several interviewees' comments highlight the importance of various personal dispositions to their professional judgments. A nurse, a physician, and an investigator mentioned forms of intuition ("Sometimes I hear that inner 'little voice.' I listen to the 'unspoken'"); trusting in their own judgment ("... at some point, you have to trust yourself"); and awareness of personal limits and others' contributions ("You consult a colleague; you always find someone who has more experience than you"). They all expressed their desire to reach the truth, to be just, and to use these dispositions throughout the evaluation process to benefit all concerned stakeholders. All interviewees wanted to serve others well and used their unique combination of these dispositions to produce credible judgments they hoped would serve their associates well. As House reminds us, "Credibility is a function of the evaluator as well as the evaluation" (p. 255).

The production of a credible judgment is a complex process achieved through the combination of evaluator and stakeholder characteristics addressing all the elements. The contributions of the professionals and their stakeholders are intertwined as they share their values and perspectives.

NEW DIRECTIONS FOR EVALUATION • DOI: 10.1002/ev

These are influenced by the professional's dispositions. And through their interactions or dialog, all participants clarify the problems or questions and generate and analyze information. Eventually, the professional reaches a judgment by making an argument that is judged as relatively credible by all participants because they view it as properly developed and communicated. Experiences described in each of the 27 cases we studied illustrate this point. The summarized testimony of a sheriff, shared below, illustrates how all the elements function together when a professional makes a credible evaluative judgment.[1]

> I intercepted a vehicle because [the registration] was outdated. The man inside was about forty years old, with three children inside. A quick investigation informed me that he lost his license in June, for unpaid fines. The law is clear in this case: it's the seizure of the vehicle for a period of 30 days and a fine of $438. With the towing of the car, we are talking costs of about $1,000. Some cops wouldn't wrack their brains over this matter and would follow the law. I talked to the man, who showed good manners. The man explained to me that he doesn't usually take this vehicle, which is plated in the name of his wife. But he had an emergency that morning. His wife was at work, and he wanted to bring their sick baby to the clinic. Indeed, there is a little baby on the back bench who doesn't seem to feel well, and we are near a clinic. I have kids of my own [and understand]. I confirmed his statements with his wife. So in this situation, I didn't have the car towed nor give him a citation because I thought it would be the children and his wife who would pay the price. I thought that it was useless to [push him] even more. I saw him a few days later, and he was sitting on the passenger side.

House (1980) acknowledged and addressed the interrelatedness of elements involved in making a credible evaluation judgment by combining truth, justice, and beauty criteria into his definition of validity. The story above unpacks House's ideas by illustrating how all the elements were present and interrelated in the sheriff's evaluation judgment, which enhanced its credibility for him and for the other participants. The sheriff could exercise his discretion in this case (Element 2), and he evaluated at first glance that the driver was a "good guy" (Element 6). He gradually developed his argument based on facts (Element 1), and not only on the protocol of the law (Element 2). Indeed, he considered the man's attitude, the information he and his wife gave, and some observations he made (Elements 3 and 4). Then he developed an argument justifying his decision based on his own criteria and his expectations of the values of his supervisors, colleagues, and the driver (Elements 3 and 5). From the start, this officer demonstrated special dispositions (Element 6). Indeed, he could have simply applied the law (Element 2) but he wanted to be fair and took the time to build a case, even though he knew that some of his colleagues "wouldn't wrack their brains over this matter and would [just] follow the law." He was aware that full enforcement of the law would be a huge imposition on this family, but being lenient would not constitute malpractice on his part. He wanted to do more than just mechanically apply the law and searched for a judgment (Elements 4 and 5) that would meet the legal requirements while giving the suspect the best options for the future.

Conclusion

This chapter summarizes research that generated an empirical and descriptive model of a process to produce a credible evaluation judgment. It was represented by six elements. Citing patterns discovered through analysis of examples from case studies of 27 professionals in many areas, we linked their experiences to House's framework regarding truth, beauty, and justice as foundations for validity. This research provides descriptive evidence that supports House's vision after more than three decades and expands the transferability of his theory to a wide variety of professions, in addition to professional evaluators. Hopefully, these results and discussion of them and the emerging model will invite professionals to reflect upon ways to improve their own evaluative judgments.

Note

1. In our commentary that follows the quote, the elements are identified by numbers, 1–6, to facilitate the reader seeing our interpretation.

References

Brehmer, B., & Joyce, C. R. B. (Eds.). (1988). *Human judgment: The social judgment theory view*. Amsterdam, Netherlands: North-Holland.

Charmaz, K. (2002). Qualitative interviewing and grounded theory analysis. In J. F. Gubrium & J. A. Holstein (Eds.), *Handbook of interview research: Context & method* (pp. 675–694). Thousand Oaks, CA: Sage.

Chelimsky, E. (2006). The purposes of evaluation in a democratic society. In I. F. Shaw, J. C. Greene, & M. M. Mark (Eds.), *The Sage handbook of evaluation* (pp. 33–55). Thousand Oaks, CA: Sage.

Chen, H. T. (2005). *Practical program evaluation: Assessing and improving planning, implementation, and effectiveness*. Thousand Oaks, CA: Sage.

Cooksey, R. (1996). *Judgment analysis: Theory, methods, and applications*. New York, NY: Academic Press.

Cousins, J. B., & Shulha, L. M. (2008). Complexities in setting program standards in collaborative evaluation. In N. Smith & P. R. Brandon (Eds.), *Fundamental issues in evaluation* (pp. 139–158). New York, NY: Guilford.

Donaldson, S. I., Christie, C. A. & Mark, M. M. (Eds.) (2009). *What counts as credible evidence in applied research and evaluation practice?* Thousand Oaks, CA: Sage.

Einhorn, H. J., Kleinmuntz, D. N., & Kleinmuntz, B. (1979). Linear regression and process-tracing models of judgment. *Psychological Review, 86*, 465–485. doi: 10.1037/0033-295X.86.5.465

Ericsson, K. A., & Simon, H. A. (1993). *Protocol analysis: Verbal reports as data.* Cambridge: MIT Press.

Fitzpatrick, J., Christie, C. A., & Mark, M. M. (2009). *Evaluation in action.* Thousand Oaks, CA: Sage.

Gilgun, J. F. (2001). Grounded theory and other inductive research methods. In B. A. Thyer (Ed.), *The handbook of social work research methods* (pp. 345–364). Thousand Oaks, CA: Sage.

Guba, E. G. (1972). The failure of educational evaluation. In C. H. Weiss (Ed.), *Evaluating action programs: Readings in social action and education* (pp. 250–266). Boston, MA: Allyn and Bacon.

Guba, E. G., & Lincoln, Y. S. (1989). *Fourth generation evaluation.* Thousand Oaks, CA: Sage.

Hammond, K. R., Stewart, T. R., Brehmer, B., & Steinman, D. O. (1975). Social judgment theory. In M. F. Kaplan & T. A. Schwandt (Eds.), *Human judgment and decision processes* (pp. 271–312). New York, NY: Academic Press.

House, E. R. (1979). Coherence and credibility: The aesthetics of evaluation. *Educational Evaluation and Policy Analysis, 1,* 5–17. doi:10.3102/01623737001005005

House, E. R. (1980). *Evaluating with validity.* Beverly Hills, CA: Sage.

House, E. R. (1995). Putting things together coherently: Logic and justice. In D. M. Fournier (Ed.), *New Directions for Evaluation: No. 68. Reasoning in evaluation: Inferential links and leaps* (pp. 33–48). San Francisco, CA: Jossey-Bass. doi:10.1002/ev.1018

House, E. R. (2010, November). *A conversation with Ernest House.* Paper presented at the Annual Conference of the American Evaluation Association, San Antonio, CA.

House, E. R. & Howe, K. R. (1999) *Values in evaluation and social research.* Thousand Oaks, CA: Sage.

Hurteau, M., Houle, S., Marchand, M.-R., Ndinga, P., Guillemette, F., & Schleifer, M. (2012). Les processus de production et de crédibilisation du jugement en evaluation. In M. Hurteau, S. Houle, & F. Guillemette (Eds.), *L'évaluation de programme axée sur le jugement crédible* (pp. 77–99). Québec, Canada: Les Presses de l'Université du Québec.

Hurteau, M., Houle, S., & Mongiat, S. (2009). How legitimate and justified are judgments in program evaluation? *Evaluation, 15,* 309–317. doi:10.1177/1356389009105883

Hurteau, M., Valois, P., & Boissiroy, A. (2010). Le jugement crédible dans le contexte de l'évaluation de programme? *Revue canadienne en évaluation de programme, 25,* 83–101. Retrieved from http://evaluationcanada.ca/secure/25-2-083.pdf

Kleinmuntz, B. (Ed.). (1968). *Formal representation of human judgment.* New York, NY: Wiley

Lincoln, Y. S., & Guba, E. G. (1985). *Naturalistic inquiry.* Beverly Hills, CA: Sage.

Patton, M. Q. (1997). *Utilization-focused evaluation: The new century text* (3rd ed.). Thousand Oaks, CA: Sage.

Schreiber, R. S. (2001). The "how to" of grounded theory: Avoiding the pitfalls. In R.S. Schreiber, & P.N. Stern (Eds.), *Using grounded theory in nursing* (pp. 55–83). New York, NY: Springer.

Schwandt, T. A. (2002). *Evaluation practice reconsidered.* New York, NY: Peter Lang.

Schwandt, T. A. (2009). Toward a practical theory of evidence for evaluation. In S. I. Donaldson, C. A. Christie, & M. M. Mark (Eds.), *What counts as credible evidence in applied research and contemporary evaluation practice* (pp. 197–212). Thousand Oaks, CA: Sage.

Scriven, M. (1980). *The logic of evaluation.* Inverness, CA: Edgepress.

Scriven, M. (1995). The logic of evaluation and evaluation practice. In D. M. Fournier (Ed.), *New Directions for Evaluation: No. 68. Reasoning in evaluation: Inferential links and leaps* (pp. 49–70). San Francisco, CA: Jossey-Bass. doi:10.1002/ev.1019

Smith, N. L. (2011, November). *Emergent, investigative evaluation: Theory, development and use in evaluation practice.* Paper presented at the Annual Conference of the American Evaluation Association, Anaheim, CA.

Stake, R. E. (2011, May). *Evaluation's generations: Veneration, vituperation, or simply divestiture.* Opening conference paper presented at the Annual Conference of the Canadian Evaluation Association, Edmonton, Canada.

Strauss, A., & Corbin, J. (1998). *Basics of qualitative research: Techniques and procedures for developing grounded theory.* Thousand Oaks, CA: Sage.

Treasury Board of Canada Secretariat (2004). *Examen de la qualité des évaluations dans les ministères et les organismes.* Retrieved from http://www.tbs-sct.gc.ca/eval/pubs/rev-exam_f.asp

MARTHE HURTEAU *is a professor in the Department of Education and Pedagogy and the academic vice-dean of the Faculty of Education at the University of Québec at Montréal.*

DAVID D. WILLIAMS *is a professor in the Instructional Psychology and Technology Department at Brigham Young University.*

Azzam, T. , & Levine, B. (2014). Negotiating truth, beauty, and justice: A politically responsive approach. In J. C. Griffith & B. Montrosse-Moorhead (Eds.), *Revisiting truth, beauty,
and justice: Evaluating with validity in the 21st century.* New Directions for Evaluation, 142,
57–70.

5

Negotiating Truth, Beauty, and Justice: A Politically Responsive Approach

Tarek Azzam, Bret Levine

Abstract

*Evaluation design and implementation are not technocratic exercises, but are
processes that require negotiations with stakeholders and careful design. This
chapter focuses on the nontechnical factors that affect these processes and discusses cases and studies to illustrate their influence. The chapter concludes by
introducing the concept of politically responsive evaluation as an organizing
frame to help evaluators consider some of the nontechnical issues that influence
evaluations.* © Wiley Periodicals, Inc., and the American Evaluation Association.

When reflecting on a way to begin this chapter, it may be most appropriate to describe an evaluation experience that sparked many of the ideas described throughout this chapter. This was an evaluation of an after-school program that aimed to increase the math skills of elementary school students in a low-socioeconomic community in Los Angeles. This program was proud of the fact that they taught math in a creative manner and aimed to increase conceptual understanding of math while focusing on certain math areas, such as geometry and measurement. As part of the evaluation, we were able to conduct a randomized control trial, in which we randomly assigned schools to treatment and control conditions. We also worked with the program on developing a measure capturing key programmatic outcomes. The program and the school district also asked us to analyze the state's standardized math test scores for the treatment and control schools as part of the evaluation, even though the program's approach and content did not fully align with this test and the program was not designed to influence these scores.

The evaluation results were mixed. The measure that focused on the program's stated outcomes and objectives indicated that control students performed as well as treatment students. These findings implied that the program had no effect on increasing the conceptual understanding of geometry and measurement. However, the state's standardized math scores showed that students in the treatment schools performed better than students in the control schools. We reported both sets of results to the program and the district, and we anticipated disappointment from the program on the null findings. To our surprise, the stakeholders from the program and district were very excited about the positive results of the standardized test scores and almost dismissed the program-specific survey results. Our team explained that the standardized test wasn't a wholly accurate measure of the program's objectives and that it should not be used as the primary measure of success since the program did not target all the content standards that the state test was capturing. We also attempted to explain that other factors that were wholly unrelated to the program could have caused these results and that heavy reliance on standardized test scores would most likely lead to disappointing results in subsequent years if and when standardized test results shifted against the treatment schools. The stakeholders from the program and district patiently listened to our concerns but eventually opted to promote the program and its success throughout the district based on the standardized test scores.

This was an unexpected and somewhat disappointing decision, and we believed that the program-specific measure should have been the primary indicator of success since it was designed and validated to capture the program-specific outcomes. This particular evaluation made us question our assumptions about validity and the factors that contribute to its achievement. In many instrument development textbooks (Crano & Brewer, 2002; Wilson, 2013), a measure must undergo a rigorous process of testing and retesting before it is deemed a *valid* measure of a particular construct. However, in the world of evaluation, the establishment of the technical quality of a measure may not be sufficient to establish its credibility to stakeholders, who are often unfamiliar with the technical merits of the information they receive and are swayed by other factors when weighing the importance of different types of information. Ignoring these external factors in an evaluation can have some unanticipated reactions (as illustrated by the earlier story) and may lead to nonuse or misuse of the evaluation.

The effects of external factors on evaluation and its credibility have been discussed in the literature since the era of modern evaluation began in the early 1960s with an influx of funding from the U.S. government (Weiss, 1997). This influx drove many newly minted scholars into the evaluation field from psychology, education, sociology, anthropology, and a host of other disciplines (Shadish, Cook, & Leviton, 1991). Many of these new evaluators began the direct translation of their training into evaluations. However, these approaches began to falter in practice due to the unique political and contextual factors that reduced their viability in the real world (Chelimsky, 1995; Cronbach et al., 1980; Datta, 2011; Weiss, 1997).

These factors include cultural norms and expectations, frequently shifting program priorities and activities, changing support structures, and differing stakeholder interests to name a few. Many of these factors can also be described in political terms, as they often emerge within a political system or process. MacDonald (1976) attempted to categorize evaluations using a political framework and offered a vision of evaluations that included the *bureaucratic* evaluation, where the evaluation is conducted for the powerful political class with no real independence or public scrutiny. There was the *autocratic* evaluation, where the evaluation is independent and technically validated by scientific standards, but its impact is often restricted to the research community. The final type is *democratic* evaluation, where information about the program and its evaluation is widely shared, multiple stakeholders are involved, and major decisions about a program are made with the awareness of how it affects different stakeholders (MacDonald, 1976). The democratic approach not only acknowledges the needs and interests of various stakeholders but also attempts to provide a fair political process to make sense of the evaluation, its findings, and implications.

House (1980) moved the democratic approach further by linking this process to validity. House (1980) described the types of relationships (personal, interpersonal, and public) that an evaluator can have with stakeholders and how they affect the criteria used to establish validity. In the personal evaluation, where "evaluator and audience are one" (House, 1980, p. 240), validity is established by utilizing appropriate methodologies and techniques in an attempt to attain a true outcome of the evaluand. The interpersonal evaluation occurs when "the evaluator works in service to the audience, but the evaluator and audience are different parties" (House, 1980, p. 240). In this situation, validity is established when the evaluation methods are technically appropriate and the findings are truthful; however, there is an added demand that the evaluation be perceived as credible and trustworthy by the audience. This added demand pushed the evaluation process away from the purely rational model of scientific inquiry (McGrath, Martin, & Kulka, 1982) and into a domain where stakeholder perceptions had to be considered. This also implied that a political process is required to determine the needs and interests of the different stakeholder constituencies. In the public relationship, the "evaluator evaluates a public program for an external audience" (House, 1980, p. 250). House (1980) stated that public evaluations should possess the qualities of the personal and interpersonal by being true and credible, but they also should be "normatively correct," meaning that the evaluation should be approached using commonly acceptable practices and designs. Thus, in public evaluation an evaluator "face[s] triple validity demands that the evaluation be true, credible, and right" (House, 1980, p. 250).

House's observations about an evaluation's validity and its relationship to stakeholder politics can be partially explained by the differences between evaluation and research (Mathison, 2008). As a result of competing stakeholder interests, logistical demands, and ethical challenges that often emerge in the real world (Campbell, 1969; Cronbach et al., 1980; Weiss 1997), evaluations more often involve pragmatic considerations than do research projects. In addition, basic and applied research are primarily concerned with generating generalizable knowledge and theory development, rather than evaluating effectiveness in a specific context (Popper, 1972). In contrast, evaluations are often conducted to determine the merit, worth, or significance of social programs (Scriven, 1991), where the primary goal is not the production of generalizable knowledge but the examination of localized program effects. Chelimsky (2013) might have stated it best when she said:

> [E]valuation practitioners ... have the task of applying principles and methods developed by theory to a world that has not always been carefully examined by theory; a world of complex, chaotic, continually moving program or policy contexts, a world of people and places that are often different with respect to tradition, social characteristics, patterns of behavior. (p. 92)

Many evaluations also aim to inform policy makers about the impact of social initiatives (Cronbach et al., 1980), and most are conducted with the hope of social betterment (Mark, Henry, & Julnes, 2000). In addition, most evaluations are conducted in applied settings where evaluator control is often negotiated with stakeholders. In these contexts, pragmatic factors can have a powerful influence on the feasibility of any evaluation design. Whereas a researcher can often control the research questions, methods, measures, implementation, and interpretation of the findings, an evaluator has to negotiate these elements with stakeholders who may have varying agendas, values, and perceptions of what is valid evidence.

These negotiations open evaluations to the political process, because the evaluator has to determine who to negotiate with, how to balance the interests of one stakeholder with those of others, and how to take into account these demands with contextual and logistical constraints to create an appropriate and valid evaluation (Greene, 1990, 2006). This process can be fraught with bias and the politics of power. Findings from a study examining the influence of stakeholders on evaluation designs suggested that a significant number of evaluators were willing to modify their original evaluation designs in response to stakeholder feedback (Azzam, 2010). These design decisions were not made to improve the technical quality of the evaluation but to improve the feasibility and reduce stakeholder resistance to the evaluation. In addition, the magnitude of the design changes correlated with the perceived power and influence of the stakeholders (i.e., the more powerful the stakeholder(s), the more changes to the evaluation design; Azzam, 2010).

Evaluators who modified their designs often stated that this was done to better capture the information needs of stakeholders[1] and hence get at the perceived truth of the program. Other evaluators believed that stakeholders wanted to focus on different programmatic elements, or wanted a deeper examination of how the program worked, and these evaluators elected to improve the evaluations credibility or perceived beauty. However, there was an imbalance in how stakeholder concerns were acted on. Many of the study's respondents disregarded the perceived needs of the least politically powerful and focused disproportionately on the needs of the most politically powerful. The study highlighted the importance of using a more democratic approach to evaluation (Howe & Ashcraft, 2005) and an increased awareness of the inequities that can creep into evaluation design decisions. This study also illustrated how a methodological design can change because of nontechnical factors to help deal with the political process occurring within evaluations. We would suggest that these changes and negotiations are meant to establish the *political credibility* of the evaluation.

Political Credibility and Politically Responsive Evaluation

House notes that validity in public domains requires truth, credibility, and normative correctness. We propose to build on House's work by attempting to describe and empirically examine the factors affecting evaluation credibility in these inherently political contexts. At its core, political credibility represents the perceived credibility of the evaluation to stakeholders and evaluators, and it is established when the evaluation is able to balance technical demands with stakeholder needs (Figure 5.1). However, the political credibility of an evaluation is not solely determined by this balance, as other factors, such as the evaluation's purpose, stakes, and characteristics can affect political credibility (Figure 5.1). It is also important to acknowledge that the term political credibility can have some negative connotations associated with it, as it may imply the submission of the evaluation to biasing political forces. The use of the term political credibility in this context aims to highlight an aspect of the evaluation process that may be neglected in practice and is meant to denote that an appropriate balance between technical demands and stakeholder needs has been achieved by engaging in a political process where both sides agree with the proposed evaluation, its subsequent implementation, and potential outcome. We would like to emphasize that the negotiation process should never result in an evaluation that is ethically dubious or that violates the program evaluation standards

Figure 5.1. Politically Responsive Evaluation Framework

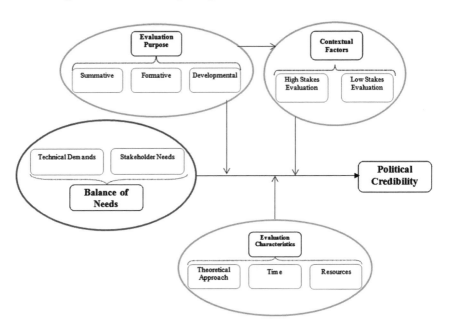

(Yarbrough, Shulha, Hopson, & Caruthers, 2011), for this type of evaluation would be invalid under any conditions.

The willingness to engage in a negotiation process with stakeholders to
achieve mutually acceptable terms to the evaluation is an initial step in carrying out a politically responsive evaluation (PRE) and establishing political
credibility (Figure 5.1). PRE combines tenants from multiple evaluation approaches and scholars. As an approach it is concerned with acknowledging
stakeholder needs and recognizing the political nature of the evaluation process. Its framing was derived from examining the contributions of Cronbach
et al. (1980), Chelimsky (1995, 1987), Greene (1990), House (1993, 1980),
Palumbo (1987), Patton (1987, 1997), and Weiss (1987, 1997). All these
scholars have described the political factors that can directly influence the
evaluative process and have consistently urged the evaluation community
to acknowledge its presence, while offering various suggestions for antici-
pating and addressing this political influence. PRE attempts to organize and
build on these observations by offering a framework that highlights the critical factors affecting the political credibility of an evaluation (Figure 5.1).
The PRE framework is primarily concerned with the balance between technical demands and stakeholder needs, and if this balance is attained, then
the evaluation achieves political credibility. One way to envision political
credibility is to view technical demands and stakeholder needs sitting on
opposite ends of a balance board. On the one end of the board are evalu-

ations that are designed solely by the evaluator with little input or influence from stakeholders. These evaluations may appear technically strong; however, they may not be politically credible to stakeholders because they were designed with little or no regard for the needs and interests of stakeholders. On the other end of the board are evaluations where stakeholders have almost complete control of the evaluation process and are able to select the measures, set the standards, and in some cases conduct the analysis and interpretation. These evaluations may have serious technical compromises and would likely suffer from reduced political credibility when reviewed in a public arena.

The balancing point between these two ends is where political credibility is achieved, and the fulcrum of the balance board can be moved or moderated by factors, such as the evaluation's purpose (summative/formative/developmental), context (high-/low-stakes evaluation), and evaluation characteristics (funding, approach, and time) (Figure 5.1). The purpose of the evaluation can influence this balance by placing more emphasis on one end over the other. For example, a summative evaluation may require more technical emphasis to achieve broader political credibility, while a formative or developmental evaluation may emphasize stakeholder needs to help ensure that findings are perceived as credible and useful for stakeholders interested in improving or developing their programs. Contextual factors can also influence this balance, and even though there are many factors that can be considered, the ones that have the largest impact relate to the stakes associated with the evaluation. A low-stakes evaluation may lead to an equal emphasis on stakeholder needs and technical demands, but is also effected by the purpose of the evaluation. For example, a low-stakes formative evaluation may lead to a stronger regard for stakeholder needs, while a high-stakes formative evaluation may decrease the emphasis on stakeholder needs. In contrast, a high-stakes summative evaluation may result in very little emphasis on stakeholder needs, and a dramatic increase in technical demands when compared to a low-stakes summative evaluation. Finally, the evaluation's characteristics can also affect political credibility, as the evaluation resources or the evaluator approach may not be appropriate to establish the needed balance between technical demands and stakeholder needs. For example, an evaluation may not be able to respond to stakeholder needs or demands due to lack of resources or time, and this may eventually reduce the evaluation's overall political credibility (Figure 5.1).

The general process of attaining this balance can be derived from existing evaluation approaches. For example, Patton's (2012) Utilization Focused Evaluation approach contains many relevant suggestions for attaining political credibility, such as gaining stakeholder buy-in for the evaluation questions, methods, and measures used, listening to stakeholder concerns, and working to build a feasible evaluation within logistical constraints. These are all steps that would increase the political credibility of an evaluation and its potential for use if these activities were not to take the evaluator too far from technical quality. Weiss's approach to evaluation would require a different tactic to achieving political credibility and its potential for evaluation influence. Weiss (1997) conducted many large federally funded evaluations of social programs, and the results of her evaluations are often reviewed with scrutiny by various interest groups. The steps needed to establish the political credibility of her evaluations would require the fulcrum of the balance beam to emphasize technical demands that would likely withstand criticism and the test of time as new policy cycles evolve; the information gained from the evaluation would spread and influence policy decisions at a later point in the cycle.

Both Patton's and Weiss' approaches share some common steps to help achieve political credibility. These steps include the conduct of a political scan within the environment as negotiations over questions, methods, and measures are occurring. This scan should remain ongoing throughout the evaluation and take particular note of the stakes involved in the evaluation, the potential winners and losers, who is at the table and who is absent, the true purpose of the evaluation, and the resources in terms of time and money that are directed toward the program and its evaluation. Ideally, this process would help the evaluator understand the political environment that stakeholders occupy and may help them avoid asymmetrical power relationships and promote inclusion of all stakeholder groups (Howe & Ashcraft, 2005).

Informed by the political scan, evaluators would need to take a politically responsive approach that (a) acknowledges the political nature of the evaluation process, (b) identifies stakeholder interests and needs, (c) seeks input from a variety of stakeholders on issues related to the evaluation process, and (d) accounts for these various demands throughout the evaluation process. The PRE process should be part of the question selection, method design, instrument development, results interpretation, and dissemination. To establish and maintain balance between stakeholder needs and technical demands, the evaluator has to negotiate throughout the evaluation. If these negotiations should fail, it would reduce the political credibility of the entire evaluation and decrease the evaluation's relevance, even if the evaluation remains technically valid.

We hope that PREs can help evaluators focus on the beauty and justice elements of House's (1980) truth, beauty, and justice conceptualization of evaluation practice. The beauty may be achieved as evaluators consider politically responsive approaches for disseminating and communicating the relevance of the evaluation's questions, methods, and findings. For an evaluation to influence its targeted stakeholders, it should be presented in a compelling and beautiful form that is appropriate to different stakeholder needs. In terms of justice, a political responsiveness evaluation can potentially help evaluators acknowledge the political repercussions of their decisions. This awareness may lead some to recognize and identify patterns of injustice in their evaluations and interactions with stakeholder groups. This reflection process may push evaluators to work toward rectifying these injustices through their evaluations.

Politically Responsive Evaluation Cases

A successful political responsive evaluation was demonstrated by the abstinence only evaluation conducted by Mathematica Policy Research (Trenholm et al., 2007). In interviews about this particular evaluation, the lead evaluators acknowledged that this was a high-stakes evaluation with summative implications (Brandon, Smith, Trenholm, & Devaney, 2010). The evaluators openly acknowledged this fact during the course of the evaluation and began the process of finding the balance between the technical demands of the evaluation and the interests of various stakeholder groups. The evaluation team engaged multiple stakeholders, including antiabstinence groups, proabstinence groups, and policy makers and requested that they express their concerns about the program and the design of the evaluation. Once these concerns were identified the evaluation team attempted to resolve them by making appropriate changes to the design. For example, in Brandon et al. (2010), the evaluators stated "we made two important decisions that addressed the legitimate concerns expressed by abstinence supporters, as well as to satisfy the evaluation objectives, and as a result we largely succeeded in getting buy-in from the broad range of stakeholders" (p. 527).

The evaluators also maintained the political credibility of the methods by forming a "technical work group" (TWG) with stakeholder groups who represented the scope of debates around the abstinence-only programs. The TWG worked with the evaluation team to deal with methodological and measurement concerns that emerged as the evaluation was implemented. This group helped ensure that the balance between technical demands and stakeholder needs was achieved and provided the evaluation team with the opportunity to explain to the group members the strength and limitation of the evaluation design and maintain their support of the methods and measures. This particular endeavor helped to increase the political credibility of the evaluation since potential opponents of the evaluation were part of the group helping to develop the evaluation. This evaluation had a great deal of political credibility, and few groups were able to argue against the findings, because the evaluation was able to maintain a balance and design an evaluation that could survive in a high-stakes summative environment. The evaluation's findings also accomplished much in terms of use, and they were a major contributing factor to policy changes at the Federal level.

In some instances in which stakeholder interests are entrenched, an evaluation's political credibility may never be established even with persistent efforts to be responsive to stakeholder needs. In a Department of Defense (DOD) evaluation, Chelimsky (2007) was entrenched in a high-stakes summative evaluation with a very hostile stakeholder. Using a research synthesis method, Chelimsky found major gaps in the information provided to policy makers from the DOD regarding its chemical weapons arsenal and capabilities. This evaluation revealed that previous DOD information and assertions about their program were based on unsubstantiated claims from the authors rather than actual evidence or data. Due to the sensitive nature of offensive chemical arms policy, the DOD had never faced any scrutiny on the quality and accuracy of the information they provided to outside policy makers. The DOD not only rejected the results from the evaluation but also attacked the credibility and, more importantly, the methodology, of the evaluation. Chelimsky (2007, p. 29) cited that the DOD claimed that the evaluation was nothing more than a "literature review." The technical quality of the evaluation design was appropriate, as the findings were pulled from reports and synthesized to show a consistent pattern of unsupported claims about the state of offensive chemical arms. However, the methods and their findings had almost no political credibility with the DOD, as the findings discredited their assertions on the topic.

Chelimsky (2007) sought to address this issue, and a letter was written to the DOD describing the benefits of the evaluation, the potential impact of the data, and how the evaluation was much more than a literature review. This step aimed to highlight the technical merits of the evaluation in the face of stakeholder opposition and was an effort to respond to stakeholder concerns. However, the DOD appeared to ignore all potential benefits of the evaluation. It was only after five years, intense political pressure, and eight more evaluations, that the DOD requested a review panel to reaffirm the methodological consistencies with the evaluation. The four-person panel took five months to confirm that Chelimsky's analysis was correct about the state of chemical weapons information, and that the DOD had failed to accept results from the evaluation.

Initial Empirical Examination

In an attempt to empirically examine the PRE framework and the effects of high-stakes summative situations on political credibility, we conducted a study that manipulated the type of data stakeholders viewed, and the stakes they were placed in (Azzam & Levine, Forthcoming). This simulation study was based on the experiences described earlier in this chapter in which two different measures were used to evaluate a program implemented within a school district. The first measure was a "standardized state test" and was described as the least technically valid for the program, since it did not specifically measure the program's intended outcomes. However, the measure was presented as important for the district, and hence was more politically valued by the district stakeholders. The second measure was a validated exam that was developed specifically to measure the program's outcomes. This "validated evaluator measure" was the most technically valid for judging the program's effectiveness because it was very aligned with the outcomes of interest, but it had less political relevance for the district.

The study had two independent variables that were manipulated, the stakes of the context, and the results from the different measures. In the high-stakes condition, participants were told that they were part of a committee that decided the fate of the program and that the committee vote was split: two votes to adopt the program and two votes to reject the program. Study participants in this high-stakes condition were asked to cast the *deciding* vote on whether to adopt the program or defund it. In the low-stakes condition, the participants were told that they were one of many votes on the program's fate, and they were not aware of how others voted.

The results from the two measures (standardized state test and validated evaluator measure) were also manipulated. Results from each of the two measures were categorical (high or low), which yielded four different conditions for this independent variable. The most interesting results arose from the two conditions in which the measurements contradicted each other (i.e., high standardized test score vs. low validated test score and low standardized test score vs. high validated test score), so that participants had to rely on either the state standardized test or the validated evaluation measure to make their decisions.

Participants were randomly assigned to these conditions, and after reading the results they were asked to rate the program's performance. After the performance was rated, the participants used a Likert scale to indicate whether they would recommend the adoption of the program. The results showed that participants were heavily influenced by the validated evaluation measure when they were asked to *rate* the program's performance, so that in conditions where the program performed poorly on the state standardized measure and well on the validated evaluation measure (regardless of the high/low-stakes manipulation), participants rated the program highly, and vice versa. However, there was a significant interaction when it came to their decisions on the program's future.

In the low-stakes condition, participants generally voted to reject the program when the validated evaluation measure results were negative and to accept the program when this measure was positive. Their decision making was heavily influenced by the evaluator measure. However, in the high-stakes condition, participants relied more on the state standardized test and increased their support of the program when this measure showed positive results and decreased their support of the program when the state standardized test was negative, even though the validated evaluator measure was positive (Azzam & Levine, Forthcoming). This was irrespective of their ratings of the program's *performance*.

These findings lend empirical support to the notion that political factors have as much influence as technical factors on rational decision making. This offers evidence that the technical merits of a design or instrument may not be sufficient to ensure that rational or reliable decisions are made from the evaluation results. This also supports House's (1980) observation that it may not be enough to focus on the technical quality of an evaluation, but that the evaluators should consider the political credibility of the evaluation as a critical piece to establishing validity. This study also highlights the need to be politically aware and responsive when conducting high-stakes summative evaluations.

Conclusion

The concepts of PRE and political credibility are ripe for future research. The study described in this chapter (Azzam & Levine, Forthcoming) was an initial step toward understanding the relationship between contextual factors (i.e., the stakes of an evaluation) and the political credibility of an evaluation. Subsequent studies could examine how varying stakeholder perspectives affect the political credibility of methods, measures, and findings. Research could also be conducted on the potential relationship between political credibility and evaluation utilization, to see if increased political credibility increases the potential for use. There are also opportunities to study how political credibility could be established during the different stages of the evaluation, assuming that different factors may have varying influence as the evaluation progresses (e.g., question selection stage may require different steps to validate politically when compared to methodological design). These investigations can contribute to our understanding of how the political process surrounding evaluations can be recognized and used to design evaluations that are valid using technical and nontechnical standards.

Note

1. Stakeholders in this study were comprised of decision makers, implementers, and recipients.

References

Azzam, T. (2010). Evaluator responsiveness to stakeholders. *American Journal of Evaluation, 31*, 45–65. doi:10.1177/1098214009354917

Azzam, T., & Levine, B. (Forthcoming). *Political credibility: An empirical examination of its influence on measurement* [Working title]. Manuscript in preparation.

Brandon, P. R., Smith, N. L., Trenholm, C., & Devaney, B. (2010). Evaluation exemplar: The critical importance of stakeholder relations in a national, experimental abstinence education evaluation. *American Journal of Evaluation, 31*, 517–531. doi:10.1177/1098214010382769

Campbell, D. T. (1969). Reforms as experiments. *American Psychologist, 24*(4), 409–429.

Chelimsky, E. (1987). The politics of program evaluation. *Society, 25*, 24–32. doi:10.1007/BF02695393

Chelimsky, E. (1995). The political environment of evaluation and what it means for the development of the field. *American Journal of Evaluation, 16*, 215–225. doi:10.1177/109821409501600301

Chelimsky, E. (2007). Factors influencing the choice of methods in federal evaluation practice. In G. Julnes & D. J. Rog (Eds.), *New Directions for Evaluation: No. 113. Informing federal policies on evaluation methodology: Building the evidence base for method choice in government sponsored evaluation* (pp. 13–33). San Francisco, CA: Jossey-Bass. doi:10.1002/ev.213

Chelimsky, E. (2013). Balancing evaluation theory and practice in the real world. *American Journal of Evaluation, 34*(1), 91–98.

Crano, W. D., & Brewer, M. B. (2002). *Principles and methods of social research.* New York, NY: Psychology Press.

Cronbach, L. J., Ambron, S. R., Dornbusch, S. M., Hess, R. D., Hornik, R. C., Phillips, D. C., ... Weiner, S. S. (1980). *Toward reform of program evaluation.* San Francisco, CA: Jossey-Bass.

Datta, L.-E. (2011). Politics and evaluation: More than methodology. *American Journal of Evaluation, 32*, 273–294. doi:10.1177/1098214011400060

Greene, J. C. (1990). Technical quality versus responsiveness in evaluation practice. *Evaluation and Program Planning, 13*, 267–274. doi:10.1016/0149-7189(90)90057-4

Greene, J. C. (2006). Evaluation, democracy, and social change. In I. F. Shaw, J. C. Greene, & M. M. Mark (Eds.), *The sage handbook of evaluation* (pp. 118–140). Thousand Oaks, CA: Sage.

House, E. R. (1980). *Evaluating with validity.* Beverly Hills, CA: Sage.

House, E. R. (1993). *Professional evaluation: Social impact and political consequences.* Newbury Park, CA: Sage.

Howe, K. R., & Ashcraft, C. (2005). Deliberative democratic evaluation: Successes and limitations of an evaluation of school choice. *Teachers College Record, 107*, 2275–2298. doi:10.1177/109821400402500403

MacDonald, B. (1976). Evaluation and the control of education. In D. Tawney (Ed.), *Curriculum evaluation today: Trends and implications* (pp. 125–136). London, UK: MacMillan Education.

Mathison, S. (2008). What is the difference between evaluation and research and why do we care? In N. Smith & P. Brandon (Eds.), *Fundamental issues in evaluation* (pp. 183–196). New York, NY: Gilford Press.

Mark, M. M., Henry, G. T., & Julnes, G. (2000). *Evaluation: An integrated framework for understanding, guiding, and improving policies and programs.* New York, NY: Jossey-Bass.

McGrath, J. E., Martin, J., & Kulka, R. A. (1982). *Judgment calls in research.* Beverly Hills, CA: Sage.

Palumbo, D. J. (Ed.). (1987). *The politics of program evaluation.* Newbury Park, CA: Sage.

Patton, M. Q. (1987). Evaluation's political inherency: Practical implications for design and use. In D. Palumbo (Ed.), *The politics of program evaluation* (pp. 100–145). Beverly Hills, CA: Sage.

Patton, M. Q. (1997). *Utilization-focused evaluation: The new century text* (3rd ed.). Thousand Oaks, CA: Sage.

Patton, M. Q. (2012). A utilization-focused approach to contribution analysis. *Evaluation, 18*, 364–377.

Popper, K. R. (1972). *Objective knowledge: An evolutionary approach.* Oxford: Clarendon Press.

Scriven, M. (1991). *Evaluation thesaurus.* Thousand Oaks, CA: Sage.

Shadish, W. R., Cook, T. D., & Leviton, L. C. L. (1991). *Foundations of program evaluation.* Newbury Park, CA: Sage.

Trenholm, C., Devaney, B., Fortson, K., Quay, L., Wheeler, J., & Clark, M. (2007). *Impacts of four title V, section 510 abstinence education programs*. Princeton, NJ: Mathematica Policy Research.

Weiss, C. H. (1987). Where politics and evaluation research meet. In D. Palumbo (Ed.), *The politics of program evaluation* (pp. 47–71). Beverly Hills, CA: Sage.

Weiss, C. H. (1997). *Evaluation* (2nd ed.). Upper Saddle River, NJ: Prentice-Hall.

Wilson, M. (2013). *Constructing measures: An item response modeling approach*. New York, NY: Routledge.

Yarbrough, D. B., Shulha, L. M., Hopson, R. K., & Caruthers, F. A. (2011). *The program evaluation standards: A guide for evaluators and evaluation users* (3rd ed.). Thousand Oaks, CA: Sage.

TAREK AZZAM *is an assistant professor and codirector of the Claremont Evaluation Center in the School of Social Science, Policy, & Evaluation at Claremont Graduate University.*

BRET LEVINE *is a doctoral student in evaluation and applied research methodology at Claremont Graduate University and an institutional researcher at Pitzer College.*

NEW DIRECTIONS FOR EVALUATION • DOI: 10.1002/ev

Bledsoe, K. L. (2014). Truth, beauty, and justice: Conceptualizing house's framework for evaluation in community-based settings. In J. C. Griffith & B. Montrosse-Moorhead (Eds.), *Revisiting truth, beauty, and justice: Evaluating with validity in the 21st century. New Directions for Evaluation, 142*, 71–82.

6

Truth, Beauty, and Justice: Conceptualizing House's Framework for Evaluation in Community-Based Settings

Katrina L. Bledsoe

Abstract

The goal of this chapter is to discuss House's theoretical framework of truth, beauty, and justice and its relationship to community-based evaluation and programming. Within this chapter, each area of House's triad is addressed separately. To further illustrate these points, aspects such as community systems, credibility of information, multicultural validity, coherence in reporting, and social justice are discussed. Throughout this discussion, examples highlighting the author's work with community-based evaluations, particularly in communities that are hard to reach, underserved, etc., are provided to ground these concepts in practice. Finally, the author poses questions about evaluation practice, validity, and social justice. © Wiley Periodicals, Inc., and the American Evaluation Association.

Whenever I reread the work of Ernest House, I am reminded how much of a "quiet storm" he has caused in the field of evaluation. House is passionate about the evaluative process, and I have always thought that his work resonated with the interpretevist and constructivist nature of the process.

This chapter emerges out of a presentation given at the 2010 American Evaluation Association's (AEA) annual conference on *Evaluation*

Quality. Then-president Leslie Cooksey challenged the membership to consider the quality of evaluation at every stage using House's (1980) seminal book, *Evaluating with Validity* as a framework. In particular, she implored members to focus on three aspects: truth, beauty, and justice. I had the honor of presenting on a panel presided by the issue editors. That panel instigated a conversation between the authors of this issue in trying to articulate how House's work continues to influence the field. I was asked to consider how his work manifests in community settings. Specifically, I wanted to think about what truth, beauty, and justice mean in these settings, how they are defined, how they present in practice, and their order of priority. After working in a variety of ethnic and socioeconomic status environments, I realize that each is a key component in community-based settings, and difficult to disengage from the other.

The goal of this chapter is to further discuss House's work and its relationship to community-based evaluation, specifically focusing on historically disadvantaged groups. Within this chapter, I address each area of House's triad, while discussing key experiences in conducting community-based evaluations, particularly in communities that are hard to reach and underserved.

Brief Overview of *Evaluating with Validity*

House's theoretical framework continues to inspire the field (House, 1980). In his classic book, he takes the reader through a philosophical and self-reflective journey of how evaluation is and should be conducted. House has always had a focus on fairness; his work in deliberative democratic evaluation emphasized bringing the democratic process to evaluation to better secure increased accuracy and *validity* in results (House & Howe, 2000). So it makes sense that his discussions on the standards of truth, beauty, and justice also have a foundation in fairness. But he also indicated that if a choice must be made it is justice that must come first in the evaluation, then truth, and then beauty. In my 2010 presentation, I posited that all three aspects needed to be present in a good community-based evaluation, especially to insure the utilization of results. I believed that all three have equal weight, and are intricately intertwined with one another. Since that time, however, I have read about and have had experiences that have caused me to think deeply about each tenet, and how they present in community-based settings. To begin the discussion, let me provide a brief background on what I consider the nature of community-based settings.

What Is the Nature of Communities?

To understand why communities are unique, one must understand the complex system that exists. Denotatively, communities are defined as a social unit of any size that shares common values, social ties, and share common perspectives (MacQueen et al., 2001). I define *community-based* as the *grounding* of the community in its unique environment, context-driven values, beliefs, norms, and behaviors. Communities are unique in their own right, responsive to and developed in accordance with, the environment in which they reside. I think of Uri Bronfenbrenner's ecological theory of development (Bronfenbrenner as cited in Myers, 2011) as a framework by which to understand how they function.

Bronfenbrenner's multilevel ecosystem has five interconnected systems. The *microsystem* refers to the institutions and groups that most immediately and directly impact the individual, such as families, neighbors, schools, peers, and neighborhoods. The *mesosystem* refers to relationships between microsystems or connections between contexts. The mesosystem is most concerned with interrelationships, such as how a child's home life might affect the way they perform at school and how that child's school experience may impact their behavior in the home environment. The *exosystem* focuses on the connection between the individual and an indirect, possibly nonactive setting. For example, a drug prevention program for adolescents might indirectly affect those young people who are not involved in the program through adolescents who *are* involved. The *macrosystem* is focused on the culture in which the individuals reside. Cultural context indicators include but are not limited to socioeconomic status, gender, race, and ethnicity. Bronfenbrenner contends that the macrosystem is dynamic and evolves over time, with each generational and cultural shift. Finally, the *chronosystem* focuses on the overarching environment, and cultural and historical perspectives and circumstances (Bronfenbrenner as cited in Myers, 2011).

I am partial to this model because it demonstrates how multilevel and multifaceted communities are as systems, and how they are influenced by incidents, relationships, contexts, and the environment. Thus, communities have multiple perspectives, multitruths, are socially constructed, and are subject to complex and intricate relationships (Andranovich & Riposa, 1997).

As mentioned earlier, communities, while intertwined with and influenced by the environment, are also socially constructed (e.g., Guzman, 2003). Given that community members' perspectives are influenced and shaped by their experiences within their environment and context, it makes sense that those with varied histories with discrimination, subjugation, and inequitable appropriation of resources would construct attitudes and opinions that may be circumspect of the system. By extension, communities' experiences with evaluation have often mirrored their general experiences within the larger system. This is especially true for those that are most vulnerable and may have experienced a culture of historical disadvantage (Bledsoe & Hopson, 2009).

Conducting Evaluation in Community-Based Settings

Due to past experiences—some of which are past hurts—communities are more interested in sharing a primary role in the evaluative process rather than being passive (Bledsoe & Hopson, 2009). Governments, universities, and well-funded others have often dictated and stipulated the evaluative process and the degree of collaboration to which each constituent would engage. However, communities now demand much more say in the evaluation that is conducted ranging from the questions that are asked to the method design and dissemination of results. Thus, the evaluator is no longer the all-powerful, thereby equalizing the power structure between evaluator and the participant.

Communities of color, women, indigenous populations, communities of low socioeconomic status, the LGBT community (lesbian, gay, bisexual, and transgendered), and persons with disabilities (among others) have often had the least power in the evaluative relationship and have been vulnerable to unethical treatment either directly or due to neglect (Bledsoe & Hopson, 2009). Incidents such as the on-going case of Henrietta Lacks (Skloot, 2010) provide an excellent example of how communities have been disregarded in the research and evaluative process.

In the 1950s, Lacks had been diagnosed with Stage 1 cervical cancer and samples from her tumor were made available to biomedical researchers to be studied, without her or her family's permission. Although these cells have become the well-known HeLa cells that are commonly used in a variety of biomedical research studies, as recently as 2013 neither Lacks nor her immediate or extended family had been contacted about use of the cells (Silver, 2013).

Examples such as this provide historically disadvantaged communities with reason to pause; many have voiced concern that there might be further pathologizing by outside others (e.g., Bledsoe & Hopson, 2009). As a result, communities are taking control of their information beginning with the manner in which it is gathered to dissemination. These demonstrations of dominion have manifested in the form of groups such as community Tribal Councils, and community developed institutional review boards (IRBs). Thus, in addition to having to address scholarly IRBs, evaluators must now address community constructed IRBs consisting of members who would be prospective participants.

Truth

Historically evaluation has been focused on searching for both certainty and credibility (House, 1980). But House maintained that evaluation can never really be certain, only more or less credible. In an excerpt from *Evaluating with Validity*, the chapter focusing on the *Logic of the Evaluative Agreement* discusses the distinction between certainty and credibility:

NEW DIRECTIONS FOR EVALUATION • DOI: 10.1002/ev

Certainty is often defined by the best scientific methods, yet ... credibility is a term in individual psychology, i.e., a term that has meaning only with respect to an individual observer. To say that some proposition is credible is, after all, to say that it is believed by an agent who is free not to believe it, that is, by an observer who, after exercising judgment and (possibly) intuition, chooses to accept the proposition as worthy of his believing it. (House, 1980, p. 71)

This quote illustrates the juxtaposition of certainty and credibility, and it is especially poignant for communities. For example, communities look for certainty in programming, and often want programs that are evidenced-based and can be guaranteed to work for the population of interest (e.g., Fitzpatrick, 2007). However, most programs will likely only address the needs of those who *seek the services* and feel that the services offered best address their needs, based upon their specific *values*. Therefore, it must be understood that evaluation can't be expected to be a panacea (in terms of certainty) and it must address the context, community of focus, and the presiding *values* to be considered credible (e.g., Donaldson, 2009). Thus, situational and contextual factors, and community characteristics must be considered within the equation. This consideration can be difficult for funders or communities to accept especially if they have a preconceived idea of the type of evaluation needed to establish credibility. The information gathered must be credible enough to be persuasive to the audience that bothers to attend to it (Petty & Cacioppo, 1986).

Additional issues to consider in the pursuit of "truth" are the perception of objectivity of information and whether qualitative information can and should be as persuasive as quantitative data. The focus for communities is really about what is considered credible evidence by the community *itself*, driven by its unique context rather than credibility determined by others (e.g., Bledsoe & Donaldson, forthcoming). If this is the case, then questions that must be asked include "what is credible evidence?" and "which set of criteria defines credible evidence?" Bronfenbrenner's model articulates the interplay between systems and the kinds of questions that should be asked. Such questions encourage the evaluation to be inclusive of the members who may not be traditionally asked to sit at the table to make decisions for what is considered credible evidence.

To illustrate this, my team and I worked with a program designed to provide prenatal care to young low-income African American women in New Jersey. Although roll out of the program to the community was extensive, there was a low turnout of clientele. Funders and program staff assumed that the community did not want and were not appreciative of the program, and that prenatal care was not in the value system of the population. The evaluation team found that young African American mothers and mothers to be had not been asked to participate in the planning of the program or in the determination of needs. Results found that contextual, socioeconomic, political, and historical factors influenced the perceptions and reality of African American women in the city. These included a history of racism in the city, perceptions of poor treatment from the medical community, and use of cultural-specific strategies to insure prenatal care. Thus, the credibility of the program and its associated "truths" was called into question by the community and was subsequently rejected (Mertens & Bledsoe, 2013).

Validity and Truth

Validity refers to the "truth and the accurate representation of information" (Cozby & Bales, 2011, p. 86). Yet, even methods titan Donald Campbell has acknowledged that validity is imperfect; knowledge and its construction are subject to inaccuracies that might not fully correspond with the evaluand (Nagireddy, 2011). But in a Campbellian validity framework the evaluator is considered an expert observer on behalf of those "knowers" who do not have the time, knowledge, and/or inclination to observe while admittedly using herself or himself and his or her experiences as a source for guidance (Nagireddy, 2011). House would agree with Campbell in his quest for the determination of a more accurate truth, but would also understand that establishment of validity in community-based evaluative setting needs to be much more expansive and inclusive. I would suggest that validity cannot be based upon one expert knower conceptualizing on behalf of all, instead, it must be fully conceptualized by those who might hold the perception of many truths.

Chen's (2005, 2012) and Kirkhart's (2013) recent work aptly describe the dynamic nature within communities. Chen (2012) advocates a bottom up, participatory, community and contextually defined validity (which he refers to as viable validity), rather than a top-down positivistic one. In addressing validity from a bottom-up perspective, he contends that programs and by extension, evaluations will provide credible evidence, be responsive to the context, and enable external validity.

Kirkhart's (2013) work on multicultural validity addresses the issue of culture as a key component for credibility. She contends that the culture, values, people, and context *frame* validity. For Kirkhart, validity is affected by the justifications and threats of experience, the life and situational experiences of the program participants and stakeholders; relationship, the relationship between participants and places; methodology, the type of method used to uncover the truth; theory, the theoretical foundation upon which the "truth" is based; and consequences, the impacts and ramifications of the evaluation to support the truth claims.

Beauty

During the 2013 AEA conference focusing on *Evaluation Practice in the 21st Century*, House divulged that the term, *beauty* was in reference to the esteemed poet John Keats. I imagine House envisioned that *coherence and credibility* in an evaluation would be an element of beauty. In contemplating this concept, I anticipate a story (of a program, for example) that is told in a coherent cohesive manner that is persuasive and is considered credible *by the community* would be a thing of beauty. House says this is a delicate balancing act. How does the evaluator make the story dramatic enough to relay the foundation of the programming, but objective enough so that it doesn't "borderline on apathy" (House, 1980)? Stories must be carefully crafted, guided by the community's perceptions of its culture and its context. These perceptions must be carefully tempered so as not to encourage prejudices and stereotypes (Bledsoe & Hopson, 2009). Thus, beauty also seems to demand cultural competence, respect, and an open mind.

But what is meant by beauty in community-based settings? When House talks about coherence and credibility in the reporting of information, he also delineates the difference between certainty in reporting and dramatic interludes in storytelling. I often use Petty and Cacioppo's (1986) elaboration likelihood model (ELM), developed within the field of social psychology, to illustrate the interplay between context and circumstances. ELM postulates that those who are most invested in the topic are likely to centrally attend to the information presented. Those who are most invested in the topic are likely to centrally process the information presented. That is, they are more likely to be informed about the topic of interest and also likely to listen to and consider information that may not be in agreement with what they believe or want to hear. Conversely, those who are less informed (and therefore less invested) about the topic are less likely to attend to the information and instead consider peripheral and unrelated cues. Consideration of how information can be heard is important.

Funders and evaluators often wonder how to frame reports and communications to communities to be more persuasive especially when results might not be as expected (Weiss, 1997). Questions to consider are "who is the audience?" and "what questions have been answered, those determined by the community or those presented by others outside of the community?" In a recent work with a North Carolina community interested in understanding parental engagement in schools, we have determined that there are several products that will be presented to a variety of stakeholders including oral presentations highlighting anecdotal information, briefing reports for local business enterprises, and research reports for faculty and researchers. The goal is to engage each constituent group to centrally attend to and be persuaded by the information rather than to focus on peripheral cues.

Credibility and coherence in reporting would certainly extend to the ubiquitous logic model. No longer singularly linear, logic models have become more systems focused, allowing for a more in-depth understanding of the context in which the program is situated (Bledsoe, forthcoming). To capture this, logic models are more complex, multileveled, and inclusive.

Additionally, they can be interactive and address the needs of several communities. For example, my colleague Shai Fuxman and his team members at Education Development Center (Fuxman, 2013) developed several models for a health program addressing a multicultural adolescent population. The team anticipated that each group might respond differently to the program and designed logic models that were culturally relevant for Latinos, African Americans, Native Americans, and the LGBT community. By designing community-specific models the team was able to develop questions that had meaning to each constituency, and could be answered in what would be considered a credible and coherent manner by each community.

Justice

For House (1980) acknowledging that evaluation is a political activity is the first step in understanding the role of justice in evaluation. He discusses three types, utilitarianism, pluralism/intuitionism, and justice as fairness, which he suggests should be the type of justice that evaluations address (House, 1980). Utilitarianism, according to philosopher John Rawls, is focused on achieving the greatest amount of satisfaction across all individuals. According to Rawls, utilitarianism requires that there be an agreed upon standard by which quantified measures of utility can be measured (Rawls, 1971). Pluralism/intuitionism is focused on discerning which principle, desire, or value is most just. Principles are weighed against one another without a determination of a standard. Finally, Rawlsian "justice as fairness" posits that there must be an agreed upon standard, value or goal in which individuals are free to access and maximize (House, 1980).

Social justice, which is a term that is often used in work that focuses on communities that are underserved has often been compared to "justice as fairness" (Rawls, 1971). The premise of social justice is based upon the principles of equality and solidarity and maintains that a socially just society understands and values human rights, as well as recognizes the dignity of every human being, no matter what their status or station in life (e.g., Mertens, 2009). In a socially just society, the belief in the dignity of every human being and their right to exist and thrive in an *equitable* manner is the standard upon which distribution of resources and opportunities (e.g., financial and political) is based (e.g., Mertens, 2009). Thus, social justice focused evaluations address issues such as distribution of power, human rights, and discrimination.

At the time *Evaluating with Validity* was written, House noted that evaluation techniques and practices did not belong to a particular theory of justice. However in recent decades, evaluation approaches that specifically address and advocate for social justice have been developed. Certainly Lincoln and Guba's (1985) naturalistic inquiry would be considered a foundation in conducting evaluations that address social justice. Participatory approaches, such as empowerment evaluation (Fetterman & Wandersman,

2005), deliberative democratic evaluation (House & Howe, 2000), transformative evaluation (Mertens, 2009), and culturally responsive evaluation (Frierson, Hood, & Hughes, 2010) are often used to address social justice, particularly in communities where disadvantage and lack of resources have been part of the historical landscape.

For example, Merten's (2009) transformative evaluation is focused on the promotion of human rights and social justice in developing worlds. In a transformative paradigm, communities are at the table as equal partners and are an integral part to the evaluation process. The values of *all* are considered important to maximizing community growth and stability.

Like transformative evaluation, culturally responsive evaluation (Frierson et al., 2010) also addresses social justice. In a culturally responsive approach, culture and cultural context help frame the evaluation beginning with the questions asked to the dissemination of results. Its iterative process insures continued vigilance to the consideration of culture and context throughout the evaluation and beyond.

Mertens (2009) says that the consideration of culture and context is a key consideration in fostering social justice in community-based settings. The American Evaluation Association's *Public Statement on Cultural Competence in Evaluation* reminds evaluators that cultural responsiveness and competence in evaluation is imperative to insuring validity and ethical treatment in communities and to further fostering social justice (AEA, 2011). To this end, Kirkhart's (2013) culture checklist suggests that there are several aspects to consider to ensure an evaluation that is considered credible and will be used. She notes that evaluations must consider history (understanding the histories of the evaluand and the participants), location (situation of the evaluation and the evaluand geographically and culturally), power (understanding the history of inequities and prejudice), voice (including the perspectives of those who might be most marginalized), relationship (understanding the connections and relationships between entities), time (perceptions of), return (giving back to the community), plasticity (staying open to new and evolving ideas), and reflexivity (self-reflection).

As a means of illustration of Kirkhart's ideas let us return to the project focusing on parental engagement in schools (Bledsoe, 2014). The project was originally conceptualized by a group of stakeholders who have some status within the community hierarchy, and the values and goals had been set this governing board. Yet, the values, lived experiences, and perspectives of the population of focus had not been considered. Problems such as resegregation in schools, local and state budget cuts, and continued discrimination of African Americans were used to inform and frame the project. A social justice and human rights focus has been important in determining what groups are part of the evaluation team (parents and students from the population of focus), the manner in which data are collected (usually within the setting of choice for the community), and how information gathered will be disseminated (in community forums and town halls).

Conclusion

I've spent a great deal of time contemplating how truth, beauty, and justice manifest in community-based evaluative settings. Thirty years after the original release date, I am pleasantly surprised at how visionary *Evaluating with Validity* really is. One aspect I continue to wrestle with is which of the triad is most important. House proposed that in best-case scenario truth, beauty, and justice would all be integrated and that none would be prioritized. But, if a choice had to be made justice must triumph. Initially, I posited that all three could and should be accomplished. But I am conflicted about this. One part of me believes that truth, beauty, and justice are intimately intertwined and cannot be divorced from one another. But the other part agrees with House that in the event that a choice must be made, justice, and in particular social justice, must prevail. In an idealistic world, a trade-off would not need to be made. But as in life, trade-offs in evaluation are often made. If House is correct, then why is justice number one? For instance, if a program does not work in the manner deemed but adds to a community, do we focus on the "truth"? Evaluation theorist Michael Scriven (1998) would likely say that the "truth" is the program *is* valuable and worthwhile because the evaluation is based upon achieved, rather than intended, outcomes. Perhaps in this way justice is accomplished.

The acknowledgement of power of communities in the 21st century underscores the timeliness of House's work and how truth, beauty, and justice must be considered part of the cornerstone of conducting evaluation in community-based settings.

References

American Evaluation Association (AEA). (2011, April). *Public statement on cultural competence in evaluation*. Retrieved from http://www.eval.org/p/cm/ld/fid=92

Andranovich, G. D., & Riposa, G. (1997). *Doing urban research*. Thousand Oakes, CA: Sage.

Bledsoe, K. L. (2014, March). *Qualitative study on parental engagement in the Northwest Corridor: Final report*. Washington, DC: Education Development Center.

Bledsoe, K. L. (forthcoming). Qualitative inquiry in program theory-driven evaluation. In L. Goodyear, E. Barela, J. Jewiss, & J. Usinger (Eds.), *Qualitative inquiry in the practice of evaluation*. San Francisco, CA: Jossey-Bass.

Bledsoe, K. L., & Donaldson, S. I. (forthcoming). Culturally responsive theory-driven evaluation. In S. Hood, R. Hopson, K. Obeidat, & H. Frierson (Eds.), *Continuing the journey to reposition culture and cultural context in evaluation theory and practice*. Chicago, IL: Information Age Publishing.

Bledsoe, K. L., & Hopson, R. H. (2009). Conducting ethical research in underserved communities. In D. M. Mertens & P. Ginsberg (Eds.), *Handbook of ethics for research in the social sciences* (pp. 391–406). Thousand Oakes, CA: Sage.

Chen, H. T. (2005). *Practical program evaluation: Assessing and improving program planning, implementation, and effectiveness*. Thousand Oakes, CA: Sage.

Chen, H. T. (2012). The roots and growth of theory-driven evaluation: Assessing viability, effectuality, and transferability. In M. C. Alkin (Ed.), *Evaluation roots* (pp. 113–129). Thousand Oak, CA: Sage.

Cozby, P., & Bales, S. (2011). *Methods in behavioral research* (11th ed.). New York, NY: McGraw-Hill.

Donaldson, S. I. (2009). A practitioner's guide for gathering credible evidence in the evidence-based global society. In S. I. Donaldson, C. A. Christie, & M. M. Mark (Eds.), *What counts as credible evidence in applied research and evaluation practice?* (pp. 239–251). Los Angeles, CA: Sage.

Fetterman, D. M., & Wandersman, A. (2005). *Empowerment evaluation principles in practice*. New York, NY: Guilford Press.

Fitzpatrick, J. L. (2007). Evaluation of the fun with books program: An interview with Katrina Bledsoe. *American Journal of Evaluation, 28,* 522–535. doi:10.1177/1098214007306379

Frierson, H. T., Hood, S., & Hughes, G. B. (2010). A guide to conducting culturally-responsive evaluations. In J. Frechtling (Ed.), *The 2010 user-friendly handbook for project evaluation* (pp. 75–96). Arlington, VA: National Science Foundation.

Fuxman, S. (2013, June). *Culturally responsive evaluation: Practical considerations.* Paper presented at the Education Development Center Learning and Teaching Division's Research and Evaluation Community Brownbag, Waltham, MA.

Guzman, B. (2003). Examining the role of cultural competency in program evaluation: Visions for new millennium evaluators. In S. I. Donaldson and M. Scriven (Eds.), *Evaluating social programs and problems* (pp. 157–182). Mahwah, NJ: Lawrence Erlbaum Associates.

House, E. R. (1980). *Evaluating with validity.* Thousand Oaks, CA: Sage.

House, E. R., & Howe, K. R. (2000). Deliberative democratic evaluation. In K. E. Ryan & L. DeStefano (Eds.), *New Directions for Evaluation: No. 85. Evaluation as a democratic process: Promoting inclusion, dialogue, and deliberation* (pp. 3–12). San Francisco, CA: Jossey-Bass. doi:10.1002/ev.1157

Kirkhart, K. E. (2013). Advancing considerations of culture and validity: Honoring the key evaluation checklist. In S. I. Donaldson (Ed.), *The future of evaluation in society: A tribute to Michael Scriven* (pp. 129–160). Charlotte, NC: Information Age Publishing.

Lincoln, Y. S., & Guba, E. G. (1985). *Naturalistic inquiry.* Los Angeles, CA: Sage.

MacQueen, K., McLellan, E., Metzger, D., Kegeles, S., Strauss, R., Scotti, R., ... Trotter, R. (2001). What is community? An evidence-based definition for participatory public health. *American Journal of Public Health, 91,* 1929–1938. doi:10.2105/AJPH.91.12.1929

Mertens, D. M. (2009). *Transformative research and evaluation.* New York, NY: Guilford Press.

Mertens, D. M., & Bledsoe, K. L. (2013, November). *Transformative mixed methods evaluations.* Paper presented at the American Evaluation Association Annual Conference Professional Development Workshops, Washington, DC.

Myers, D. G. (2011). *Psychology* (10th ed.). New York, NY: Worth.

Nagireddy, N. R. (2011). *Evolutionary epistemology of Donald T. Campbell* (Unpublished doctoral dissertation). University of Hyderabad, India.

Petty, R., & Cacioppo, J. T. (1986). The elaboration likelihood model of persuasion. In L. Berkowitz (Ed.), *Advances in experimental social psychology* (pp. 123–205). Hillsdale, NJ: Erlbaum.

Rawls, J. (1971). *A theory of justice.* Cambridge, MA: Harvard University Press.

Scriven, M. (1998). Minimalist theory: The least theory that practice requires. *American Journal of Evaluation, 19,* 57–70. doi:10.1177/109821409801900105

Silver, M. (2013, August 16). A new chapter in the immortal life of Henrietta Lacks. *National Geographic Daily News.* Retrieved from http://news.nationalgeographic.

com/news/2013/08/130816-henrietta-lacks-immortal-life-hela-cells-genome-rebecca-skloot-nih/

Skloot, R. (2010). *The immortal life of Henrietta Lacks*. New York, NY: Crown Publishing Group.

Weiss, C. H. (1997). How can theory-based evaluation make greater headway? *Evaluation Review, 21*, 501–524. doi:10.1177/0193841X9702100405

KATRINA L. BLEDSOE *is a research scientist and senior evaluation specialist at Education Development Center, Inc.*

NEW DIRECTIONS FOR EVALUATION • DOI: 10.1002/ev

Hopson, R. K. (2014). Justice signposts in evaluation theory, practice, and policy. In J. C. Griffith & B. Montrosse-Moorhead (Eds.), *Revisiting truth, beauty, and justice: Evaluating with validity in the 21st century. New Directions for Evaluation, 142,* 83–94.

7

Justice Signposts in Evaluation Theory, Practice, and Policy

Rodney K. Hopson

Abstract

This chapter, influenced by Ernest House's conceptions of justice from his Evaluating with Validity *seminal book, offers two justice signposts in contemporary evaluation theory, practice, and policy. The justice turn in evaluation privileges issues of power, fairness, justice, and rights beyond practical and technical considerations. Cases and examples draw upon Housian notions of justice in advancing and making obvious how evaluation may contribute to more just practices, systems, and structures in our larger society.* © Wiley Periodicals, Inc., and the American Evaluation Association.

T he second part of Ernest House's (1980) seminal book, *Evaluating with Validity*, ends with important sentences following a discussion on justice. It reads below (with particular focus on the sentences in italics which are mine):

Versions of this paper were delivered at the 2010 and 2013 American Evaluation Association conferences. Acknowledgements are extended to Jennifer Greene, Stafford Hood, Jill Chouinard, and Karen Kirkhart for their review of previous versions of this manuscript. Additionally, William Rodick provided extensive editorial and formatting edits to multiple versions of this paper. Special acknowledgements are paid to the editors of the special issue, James Griffith and Bianca Montross Moorhead, and to Ernie House for his inspirational and provocative visions of the field decades ago.

[O]ne's theory of justice does not determine the type of evaluation one does. There are too many other factors influencing an evaluation than that. One's theory operates implicitly and subtly .... One's implicit conception of justice is in the long run significant .... Only a few people have the ability to artic- ulate a coherent theory of justice; their names grace the backs of books. It is not necessary for the evaluator to subscribe to one of these grand theories (each of which is deficient) or to articulate his own. *What is professionally responsible is for the evaluator to use these grand theories as signposts telling us where we are and where we want to go. They serve as guides for our direction.* (p. 136)

While House is credited with contributing significantly to notions of democracy and social justice in evaluation over the last 25 years (House, 2004; House & Howe, 2002; Kushner, 2005a, 2005b), there is a clear need for more developments recognizing how justice signposts influence evalua- tion. This chapter provides an overview of the justice-related approaches in evaluation from a Housian point of view. In providing an overview of jus- tice approaches in evaluation, the chapter extends ways of retracing eval- uation roots and building branches of justice and advancing an important and core attribute for the field (Alkin & Christie, 2004; Hopson & Hood, 2005; Kirkhart, 2010; Yarbrough, Shulha, Hopson, & Caruthers, 2011).

In keeping with the aim of this *New Directions for Evaluation* issue to ground these claims in the "implications for contemporary practice, con- fronted as it is, with challenges in balancing competing evaluation inter- ests," this chapter interweaves practice, research, and theory in illustrating how Housian notions of justice inform and influence contemporary evalu- ation. Accepting the challenge by House to use signposts to serve as guide for *where we are and where we want to go,* I provide two justice signposts for the evaluation field that his own work has influenced. The signposts are as follows:

1. Continue to expand the social justice or values branch of the evalua- tion theory tree.
2. Promote evaluation as liberating and decolonizing for the marginal- ized and underrepresented.

After brief discussions on signposts and Housian contributions to jus- tice turn in evaluation, I present a couple of justice signposts that have Housian legacies and why these signposts, taken individually and collec- tively, purport ways to build the field in 21st-century evaluation. Taken to- gether, the signposts discuss how Housian notions of evaluation quality require prioritizing and balancing to provide defensible and valid evalua- tions for stakeholders and colleagues in evaluation theory, practice, and/or research. Ultimately, this chapter provides an overview of justice-related approaches in evaluation from a Housian point of view, while integrating evaluation, democracy, and social change in larger perspective (Greene, 2006).

Signposts

The *Oxford English Dictionary* (2013) defines "signposts" (*n*) as "a sign giving information such as the direction and distance to a nearby town, typically found at a crossroads" and the *Oxford Advanced Learner's Dictionary* defines it as "a sign at the side of the road giving information about the direction and distance of places."

House's book and chapter from which the initial quote is drawn serves as signpost for the field, a sign giving information about the direction of the evaluation field on numerous topics, not just those identified in this chapter. House's (1980) preface of the book illustrates his expectation of the book as signpost:

> This book is directed at evaluators and at those who wish to achieve a better understanding of modern evaluation, of what it is and where it is going. The aim is to arrive at a more reflective practice.... The current evaluation scene is marked by vitality and disorder. The scale, ubiquity, and diversity of evaluation activities make comprehension difficult, even for those operating within the field. More alarmingly, a bad evaluation can deface a social program and injure an entire social class. The social import of evaluation is enormous; its self-understanding relatively minute. It is hoped that this book will contribute to a more complete and translucent conceptual order and to a stronger sense of moral responsibility. (p. 11)

In this case, the book is intending to illustrate, as the chapters in this edited volume purport through their consideration of relevant topics from this seminal book, that the evaluation field is in need of guides—essentially new directions—on ways to envision contemporary evaluation theory and practice, in this case related to the justice turn in evaluation.

House's Contribution to the Justice Turn in Evaluation

A starting point for understanding House's historical and contemporary contribution to the justice turn in evaluation is his work (House, 1980, 1991, 1993, 2001, 2004; House & Howe, 1999) and the more recent work of others (Greene, 2006; Mertens & Wilson, 2012). Greene (2006, p. 104) places House at the forefront of evaluation thinking and practice tied to notions of democracy and social change in its intent to address "inequities of social class and minority culture and to advance 'social justice' in the context at hand and in the broader society." His conceptions of evaluation suggest that its role should democratically advance and influence institutions, discourses, and policy directions.

NEW DIRECTIONS FOR EVALUATION • DOI: 10.1002/ev

Less concerned with logic or methodology in a vacuum, House recognizes the embeddedness of evaluation practices to social institutional and structural practices. The particular model of democratic society he favors, which evaluation can help constitute, attends to the interests of the least advantaged. The model of evaluation that emanates from this justice-oriented approach

> intentionally insures that the *interests* of all stakeholders, specifically those of the powerless and the poor, are respectfully included. And it prescribes procedures by which stakeholders' interests are articulated, shared, and advanced in evaluation, even when, or perhaps especially when, they conflict. These procedures rest on three inter-related principles: *inclusion, dialog,* and *deliberation* (Greene, 2006, p. 106).

The justice turn in evaluation that House proposes is practically concerned with the equitable participation of all interested stakeholders during the evaluation process in attempts to gather diverse, authentic interests through reasoned discussions, evidence, argument, and deliberation (Greene, 2006; Howe & Ashcraft, 2005; Stufflebeam, 2001). His notions of justice in evaluation, however, do not end with the practical aspects of participation, arguably more easily applied in everyday evaluation practice. Housian notions of justice in evaluation practice are as important at micro or local program levels as they are to larger government actions, political decision making, and policy formation.

At his 2004 address to the European Evaluation Society, House likened the overemphasis on randomized controlled trials in educational research and evaluation at governmental levels to "methodological fundamentalism" evaluation policy of the post-9/11/01 Bush era. The government's expectation and demand that all evaluations be randomized (and/or highly favored in government funding contracts, awards, and competitions) is illustrative of this evaluation policy in the United States. Beyond simply facilitating dialog and deliberation at program or policy levels, the evaluator in a Housian sense is a drum major for justice (King, 1968), where evaluations are used as ways of ensuring communication, negotiating and balancing key stakeholder powerful and competing interests, and legitimizing (or challenging) governmental or institutional actions in ways that produce common understandings and quality decisions. I illustrate how Housian contributions influence a recent evaluation of school choice policy in the Boulder (CO) Valley School District and balance a critique of larger social institutional structures at the educational level (Howe & Ashcraft, 2005).

Grounded in a deliberative democratic approach to evaluation "which adopts a relatively strong stance toward stakeholder participation and, along with this, some stance toward democratic decision making" (Howe & Ashcraft, 2005, p. 2275), the evaluation "was commissioned by the district, which perceived the need for a systematic examination of the effects of its open enrollment system following five years of rapid, unplanned growth" (Howe & Ashcraft, 2005, p. 2278). While the evaluation met the characteristics of a deliberative democratic evaluation through observance and application of its principles of stakeholder participation in the research process (i.e., focus groups, surveys, and census data were collected to illustrate the inclusive, dialogic, and to a lesser extent the deliberative aspects during the process), the theoretical underpinning of the approach "emphasizes developing political practices and institutions that mitigate power imbalances among citizens so as to permit their free and equal participation" (Howe & Ashcraft, 2005, p. 2276). The practical and technical aspects of the Boulder evaluation of school choice policy were only part of the story. What is arguably more significant in the use of deliberation were the political decision-making processes and maneuverings that took place after the report was completed. Equally significant was the impact of deliberation on Boulder Valley policy makers who were spurred by the study's conclusion about a number of important issues relevant to the study; these issues include inequities in funding, racial/ethnic stratification, skimming, and unequal opportunities for certain parents to participate in the school choice process. It is not difficult to see how, while participatory methods of data gathering facilitated authentic perspectives of key stakeholders, the larger issues at the heart of the study lie in ensuring that public good, justice, and equity were fundamental to policy formation and evaluation, contributions of a Housian turn toward justice in evaluation.

Contemporary Justice Signposts in Evaluation

What follows in the subsequent sections are the contemporary justice signposts for continued direction in the field inspired by House, collaborators, and protégés. Following the presentation of each signpost, examples and practices from the field provide for further discussion and deliberation.

Signpost 1: Continue to Expand the Social Justice or Values Branch of the Evaluation Theory Tree

If the existing evaluation theory tree represents "the trunk and three branches of the family tree," then we do not have any black or brown members in the family. John Stanfield's 1998 presidential plenary presentation at the American Evaluation Association conference reminded me not only does our own field reproduce dominance and subordination in what we study and evaluate but also in whom we heroify in the field (Stanfield, 1999).[1]

House's larger body of work, according to Alkin and Christie (2004), sits on the values branch influenced by Scriven (1967) and maybe even the Stake agendas. The values branch, as Alkin and Christie purport, "firmly establishes the vital role of the evaluator in valuing. Those on this branch

maintain that placing value on data is perhaps the most essential component of the evaluator's work" (p. 13). In positioning House on the values
branch, Alkin and Christie present House as one who challenges the utili-
tarian purpose and function of methods and some use theorists. To them,
House is more concerned with the role of the larger purpose of evaluation
and the evaluator, one concerned with decision-making toward equitable
allocation of resources. House's notion of justice-oriented evaluation is:

> never value neutral; it should tilt in the direction of social justice by specif-
> ically addressing the needs and interests of the powerless. House's evaluator
> is thus faced with the task of understanding the needs and positions of var-
> ious stakeholders, especially the needs and positions of various stakeholder
> groups, especially the poor and powerless, and of balancing this information
> with his or her perception of social justice. (Alkin & Christie, 2004, p. 41)

The first signpost recognizes there is more work to do to advance this
Housian values branch or the social justice branch (as conceived by Mertens
& Wilson, 2012). Mertens and Wilson's (2012) rethinking of the evaluation
tree incorporates a separate branch, a social justice branch, alongside methods, use, and valuing branches. House sits on this social justice branch and
this branch incorporates more than the deliberative democratic approach,
but it also includes the human rights, feminist, LGBTQ, Lat-Crit, disability,
indigenous, and critical race approaches. It is precisely these approaches
that answer John Stanfield's questions he posited at the 1998 plenary:

> The question is, how relevant are social scientists going to be in exploring
> what is really going on and developing theories and methods to fine tune such
> processes of change and transformation occurring locally, nationally, and in-
> ternationally? How do social scientists change the institutional frameworks
> of research education and certification, making them much more concerned
> with approaching anti-racism issues more from the standpoints of power and
> privilege than from deficit modeling and community outreach strategizing
> more from the standpoint of empowerment than paternalistic class or racial
> stereotyping? How do we make agencies which fund social research and gov-
> ernment agencies, nonprofit organizations, and businesses which contract
> consulting social scientists much more forward thinking rather than seeped
> in nineteenth century notions of America and of people of color as "minori-
> ties?"

Stanfield answers his own questions in the sentences that immediately
follow, offering a signpost similar to House for "those who are involved in
evaluation research examining the conventional epistemologies, theories,
and methods of their crafts and becoming much more concerned with approaching people of color in their own terms." In a critical analysis of race
and education policy in the United States, House (1999, p. 11) makes it

evident that our educational practices such as around financing, differentiated curricula, standardized testing, ability groups, while appearing to have little to do with race, instead "reveals that the policies effectively segregate, differentiate, and provide minorities with an inferior education. The operation of the system as a whole has racial consequences even if those administering it do not have that in mind." House's critique on race and education policy along with Stanfield's questions suggests that these areas of study for the evaluator concerned with justice require much more attention and consideration in ways that honor and recognize how disparate democracy exists in evaluation (Hood, 2000).

The first signpost ensures that the evaluation roots tree recognizes the ongoing legacy and historical contributions of CRE (culturally responsive evaluation) through a series of essays related to a larger project, Nobody Knows My Name project, that have been written in the last decade to restore the tradition of unrecognized African American evaluators (Frazier Anderson & Bertrand Jones, 2014; Hood, 2001; Hood & Hopson, 2008; Hood, Hopson, & Frierson, 2005; Hood, Hopson, Obeidat, & Frierson, 2014; Hopson & Hood, 2005). The core of this CRE work extends the social justice branch in the Housian justice-oriented tradition.[2] Reid E. Jackson, Rose Browne, Leander Boykin, Aaron Brown, and others conducted comprehensive evaluations in a pre-*Brown v. Board of Education* era at a time when racial segregation and inequality were the norms of the day in segregated schools in the southern part of the United States. Their work recognizes that the social justice turn requires above all a social responsibility to serve communities less fortunate, underserved, and marginalized.

Signpost 2: Develop Evaluation as a Way to Liberate and Decolonize Issues and Challenges Faced by Marginalized, Underserved, and Underrepresented

At a recent AEA presentation at the 2012 conference, a good friend and mentor chided me for advancing notions of decolonizing evaluation. He admonished my use of those concepts and thought that funders and clients would be off-put by the word "decolonizing." The paper was a presentation on a set of concepts related to evaluation in developing contexts, especially where equity-focused evaluation is promoted (Hopson, Kirkhart, & Bledsoe, 2012; Segone, 2012). The case study in this chapter was based on an ethnographic evaluation study of San education in eastern Bushmanland, Namibia, a couple of years previously (Hays, Hopson, & LeRoux, 2010). It only occurred to me after he sat down next to me that he was issuing me a challenge to clarify how and why evaluation should serve in liberating and decolonizing ways. Surely, he could not be telling me NOT to use the terms but to make clear why these liberating and decolonizing notions in the field would serve groups often marginalized and underrepresented (Kawakami, Aton, Cram, Lai, & Porima, 2007; Smith, 2012).

NEW DIRECTIONS FOR EVALUATION • DOI: 10.1002/ev

The second signpost recognizes that, much like Greene, Millett, and Hopson (2004) acknowledge, evaluation "has a liberating role to play in extricating society from this particular social construction of privilege and advantage. Given that evaluation inevitably advances certain values and interests and not others, it can either maintain and reinforce the existing system, or it can serve to challenge, disrupt, and strive to change the existing social order to one that is more equitable, and just more democratic" (pp. 102). Decolonizing or liberating notions in the field should be perceived as ways to challenge the increasing challenges faced by groups indigenous, marginalized, or underserved in the context of debilitating and colonial educational and social policies.

With respect to the San educational evaluation study, three of us as a team were contracted by a European funding agency to evaluate the educational developments and mechanisms after years of support for teacher training, curriculum development, learning materials among a group of San (or Bushmen) in Namibia, southern Africa. The evaluation had the potential elements of exposing the problematic relationships between a funder in the global north and beneficiaries in the global south who are extremely marginalized among indigenous populations worldwide.

For any one who does work in southern Africa or among indigenous groups worldwide, there is a common understanding that the San represent a particularly marginalized and indigenous group sandwiched historically between colonialism and apartheid in a changing contemporary southern Africa (Hopson & Hays, 2008). Efforts and interventions have been attempted for decades to assist the educational and social outcomes, and this was but another effort to improve the access to quality education for the group. Government and nongovernment organizations in Botswana, South Africa, and Namibia have invested funds and tried various approaches to incorporating the San into the mainstream education systems. What we see across the region for San communities is very small steps toward achieving some measure of success in the mainstream systems. While the numbers of San children accessing some schooling are going up, the dropout rates are extremely high. The San are commonly known among government officials as "the most difficult" group to work with when it comes to educational initiatives.

A report was completed based on a desk study (or literature review) and fieldwork in the region over a six-month period in 2010 by the evaluation team. Program materials and documents, correspondences, policy documents from the Ministry of Education and other nongovernmental organizations, annual reviews, and meeting minutes were examples of the materials collected during the desk study. Over 100 people were interviewed making up government officials, San education staff, principals, teachers, learners, and community persons in several regions of the country. Minimal observations of San learners in formal schools took place to get the most updated and accurate depiction of their participation in schools.

NEW DIRECTIONS FOR EVALUATION • DOI: 10.1002/ev

With an effort focused largely on improving participation in mainstream education, the evaluation reinforced that the project also attempted to provide a set of skills and opportunities. Despite the low numbers of learners who actually matriculated to postsecondary education or the number of San teachers certified and trained to teach at the primary or junior-secondary levels, it is possible that the evaluation results could suggest that this work has yielded little direct outcome for the community and there were records to suggest that the San do not achieve the same educational and social outcomes by other groups.

The evaluation team reported that approaches that focus primarily on increasing San children's participation in government schools under the existing circumstances have not been shown to be effective and, given the poor quality of these institutions and the host of well-documented problems, do not ultimately serve the interests of the San community. These approaches also do not take into account the depth of the transition process involved for the San communities and individuals in participating in the mainstream schools. In short, they neglect the root problems–and they do not work. The report noted that attempts to achieve the goals of getting more San children in Tsumkwe school, or developing more San teachers, underestimate the amount of time and support needed; they also largely neglect the traditional culture of San communities and the skills that the children and the teachers already bring with them to their educational processes. Special approaches are needed for these communities to achieve these two goals, and many other goals that the funder strives to achieve.

In the evaluation report, we argue that taking a *rights-based approach* to improving education in the Tsumkwe district is an important step to San educational development and success. In particular, the report emphasized an *indigenous rights* approach that recognizes that concern for indigenous rights is not about special rights, but about providing access to basic human rights. This rights-based approach to education is liberating and decolonizing, recognizing that rights must be the key issues addressed before any other issues are addressed. The San education evaluation example illustrates the second signpost in a justice-oriented approach to evaluation, one that recognizes that evaluators make choices about the type of values and interests they promote. Evaluation as liberating and decolonizing challenges existing social orders and situations that reinforce have-nots, those marginalized, and oppressed, by bringing to surface inequitable issues that exist in the system.

Conclusions

This chapter illustrates how and why justice signposts are influenced by Ernest House and illustrates two contemporary signposts that signal future directions of the field. In offering a space for the justice turn in evaluation,

NEW DIRECTIONS FOR EVALUATION • DOI: 10.1002/ev

House and his protégés suggest that evaluation has an important role to play in extricating and illuminating power differentials, fairness, and justice. Housian perspectives on justice ultimately recognize furthermore that "we are more than technicians" (Madison, 1992, p. 1). That is, we recognize that our craft and science requires more than attention to technicality; that there is more space for advancing and making obvious how evaluation might contribute to more democratic and just practices, policies, systems, structures, and society.

Notes

1. I take a page from James Loewen's (1995) *Lies My Teacher Told Me*, a favorite text I have used in graduate multicultural education and undergraduate social justice courses to illustrate the incredible historical role and process of making heroes in an American context.
2. In a recent paper, we acknowledge Robert Stake as pivotal in influencing evaluative inquiry of "early African American scholars and evaluators" (Hood & Hopson, 2008) though it is fair to say that House's contributions complement and conceptually ground these same social agenda and advocacy (Stufflebeam, 2001) approaches.

References

Alkin, M. C., & Christie, C. A. (2004). *Evaluation roots: Tracing theorists' views and influences.* Thousand Oaks, CA: Sage.

Frazier Anderson, P. & Bertrand Jones, T. (2014). An analysis of Love my children: Rose Butler Browne's contributions to culturally responsive evaluation. In S. Hood, R. Hopson, K. Obeidat, & H. Frierson (Eds.), *Continuing the journey to reposition culture and cultural context in evaluation theory and practice.* Greenwich, CT: Information Age Publishing.

Greene, J. (2006). Evaluation, democracy, and social change. In I. Shaw (Ed.), *Handbook of evaluation: Policies, programs and practices* (pp. 118–140). London, UK: Sage.

Greene, J., Millett, R., & Hopson, R. K. (2004). Evaluation as democratizing practice. In M. Braverman, N. Constantine, & J. K. Slater (Eds.), *Foundations and evaluation: Contexts and practices for effective philanthropy* (pp. 96–118). San Francisco, CA: Jossey-Bass.

Hays, J., Hopson, R., & LeRoux, W. (2010). *Evaluation of the NAMAS supported San Education Project in Tsumke, Otjozondjupa Region, Namibia.* Norwegian Association of Namibia San Education Project. Elverum, Norway: NAMAS

Hood, S. (2000). Commentary on deliberative democratic evaluation. In K. E. Ryan & L. DeStefano (Eds.), *New Directions for Evaluation: No. 85. Evaluation as a democratic process: Promoting inclusion, dialogue, and deliberation* (pp. 77–83). San Francisco, CA: Jossey-Bass. doi:10.1002/ev.1163

Hood, S. (2001). Nobody knows my name: In praise of African American evaluators who were responsive. In J. C. Greene & T. A. Abma (Eds.), *New Directions for Evaluation: No. 92. Responsive Evaluation* (pp. 31–44). San Francisco, CA: Jossey-Bass. doi:10.1002/ev.33

Hood, S., & Hopson, R. K. (2008). Evaluation roots reconsidered: Asa Hilliard, a fallen hero in the "Nobody Knows My Name" project, and African educational excellence. *Review of Educational Research, 78,* 410–426. doi:10.3102/0034654308321211

Hood, S., Hopson, R. K., & Frierson, H. T. (2005). *The role of culture and cultural context: A mandate for inclusion, the discovery of truth and understanding in evaluative theory and practice.* Greenwich, CT: Information Age Publishing.

Hood, S., Hopson, R. K., Obeidat, K., & Frierson, H. (Eds.). (2014). *Continuing the journey to reposition culture and cultural context in evaluation theory and practice.* Greenwich, CT: Information Age Publishing.

Hopson, R. K., & Hays, J. (2008). Schooling and education for the San (Ju|'hoansi) in Namibia: Between a rock of colonialism and the hard place of globalization. In R. K. Hopson, C. C. Yeakey, & F. Boakari (Eds.), *Power, voice and the public good: Schooling and education in global societies* (pp. 171–197). Oxford, UK: Emerald.

Hopson, R. K., & Hood, S. (2005). An untold story in evaluation roots: Reid E. Jackson and his contributions toward culturally responsive evaluation at three quarters of a century. In S. Hood, R. K. Hopson, & H. Frierson (Eds.), *The role of culture and cultural context in evaluation: A mandate for inclusion, the discovery of truth, and understanding in evaluative theory and practice* (pp. 85–104). Greenwich, CT: Information Age Publishing.

Hopson, R. K., Kirkhart, K. E., & Bledsoe, K.L. (2012). Decolonizing evaluation in a developing world: Implications and cautions for equity-focused evaluations. In M. Segone (Ed.), *Evaluation for equitable development results* (pp. 59–83). New York, NY: UNICEF.

House, E. R. (1980). *Evaluating with validity.* Beverly Hills, CA: Sage.

House, E. R. (1991). Evaluation and social justice: Where are we? In M. W. McLaughlin & D.C. Philips (Eds.), *Evaluation and education: At quarter century* (90th yearbook of the National Society for the Study of Education, Part II) (pp. 233–247). Chicago, IL: University of Chicago Press.

House, E. R. (1993). *Professional evaluation: Social impact and political consequences.* Newbury Park, CA: Sage.

House, E. R. (1999). Race and policy. *Educational Policy Analysis Archives, 7,* 1–15. Retrieved from http://epaa.asu.edu/ojs/article/view/551

House, E. R. (2001). Unfinished business: Causes and values. *American Journal of Evaluation, 22,* 309–315. doi:10.1177/109821400102200304

House, E. R. (2004, October). *Democracy and evaluation.* Keynote presentation presented at the European Evaluation Society, Berlin, Germany.

House, E. R., & Howe, K. R. (1999). *Values in evaluation and social research.* Thousand Oaks, CA: Sage.

House, E. R., & Howe, K. R. (2002). Deliberative democratic evaluation in practice. *Evaluation in Education and Human Services, 49,* 409–421. doi:10.1007/0-306-47559-6_22

Howe, K. R., & Ashcraft, C. (2005). Deliberative democratic evaluation: Successes and limitations of an evaluation of school choice. *Teachers College Record, 107,* 2274–2297. doi:10.1111/j.1467-9620.2005.00592.x

Kawakami, A., Aton, K., Cram, F., Lai, M. K. & Porima, L. (2007). Improving the practice of evaluation through indigenous values and methods: Decolonizing evaluation practice—returning the gaze from Hawai'i and Aotearoa. In P. Brandon & N. L. Smith (Eds.), *Fundamental issues in evaluation* (pp. 219–242.). New York, NY: Guilford Press.

King, M. L., Jr. (1968, February). *Drum major instinct.* Sermon given at Ebenezer Baptist Church, Atlanta, GA. Retrieved from http://mlk-kpp01.stanford.edu/index.php/encyclopedia/documentsentry/doc_the_drum_major_instinct/

Kirkhart, K. E. (2010). Eyes on the prize: Multicultural validity and evaluation theory. *American Journal of Evaluation, 31,* 400–413. doi:10.1177/1098214010373645

Kushner, S. (2005a). Qualitative control: A review of the framework for assessing qualitative evaluation. *Evaluation, 11,* 111–122. doi:10.1177/1356389005053194

Kushner, S. (2005b). Democratic theorizing: From noun to participle. *American Journal of Evaluation, 26*, 579–581. doi:10.1177/1098214005281357

Loewen, J. W. (1995). *Lies my teacher told me: Everything your American history textbook got wrong.* New York, NY: New Press.

Madison, A.-M. (1992). Editor's notes. In A.-M. Madison (Ed.), *New Directions for Program Evaluation: No. 53. Minority issues in program evaluation* (pp. 1–4). San Francisco, CA: Jossey-Bass. doi: 10.1002/ev.1596.

Mertens, D. M., & Wilson, A. (2012). *Program evaluation, theory, and practice: A comprehensive practice.* New York, NY: Guilford Press.

Scriven, M. (1967). The methodology of evaluation. In R. E. Stake (Ed.), *American Educational Research Association monograph series on curriculum evaluation, 1.*

Segone, M. (Ed.). (2012). *Evaluation for equitable development results.* New York, NY: UNICEF

Smith, L. T. (2012). *Decolonizing methodologies: Research and indigenous peoples.* London, UK: Zed Books.

Stanfield, J. H. (1999). Slipping through the front door: Relevant social science evaluation in the people of color century. *American Journal of Evaluation, 20*, 415–431. doi:10.1177/109821409902000301

Stufflebeam, D. (2001). Evaluation models. In G. T. Henry (Ed.), *New Directions for Evaluation: No. 89. Evaluation models* (pp. 7–98). San Francisco, CA: Jossey-Bass. doi:10.1002/ev.3

Yarbrough, D. B., Shulha, L. M., Hopson, R. K., & Caruthers, F. (2011). *The program evaluation standards: A guide for evaluators and evaluation users* (3rd ed.). Thousand Oaks, CA: Sage.

RODNEY K. HOPSON *is a professor in the Division of Educational Psychology, Research Methods, and Education Policy and senior policy fellow in the Center for Education Policy and Evaluation in the College of Education and Human Development at George Mason University*

Montrosse-Moorhead, B., Griffith, J. C., & Pokorny, P. (2014). House with a view: Validity and evaluative argument. In J. C. Griffith & B. Montrosse-Moorhead (Eds.), *Revisiting truth, beauty, and justice: Evaluating with validity in the 21st century. New Directions for Evaluation, 142,* 95–105.

8

House With a View: Validity and Evaluative Argument

Bianca Montrosse-Moorhead, James C. Griffith, Pamela Pokorny

Abstract

Constructed in a narrative-style, this chapter provides a summary and analysis of the present issue. Chapters included in the present issue and a series of formal conversations between the issue editors and Ernest R. House serve as the building blocks for the ideas presented. These ideas include the importance of the clarity of language in evaluation, enduring issues related to validity in evaluation, and a vision for the future concerning the validity of evaluation arguments in practice and theory. © Wiley Periodicals, Inc., and the American Evaluation Association.

> *Beauty is truth, truth beauty,—that is all*
>
> *Ye know on earth, and all ye need to know.*
>
> "Ode on a Grecian Urn," John Keats

Between June and November 2013, we conducted two interviews with Ernest (Ernie) R. House. The first interview focused on the conceptual history of the validity of evaluative arguments not covered elsewhere in this issue. The second interview aimed to synthesize the current status of validity of evaluative arguments and identify new directions for evaluative argumentation in practice and theory. Each interview lasted approximately 1 hr and 30 min, with the recordings then transcribed verbatim.

Originally, in conceptualizing this chapter, the authors assumed that this last chapter would present edited transcripts from both interviews. However, due to page constraints, choices had to be made about what to include and how best to include it. The authors made the decision to focus on what they perceived to be the significant ideas emerging from the interviews: the importance of the clarity of language in evaluation, enduring issues related to validity in evaluation, and new directions for evaluating with validity. With House's assistance, while having to cut length, we tried to give justice to the original interviews, taking special care to balance truth and beauty.

Clarity of Language in Evaluation

The terms, truth, beauty, and justice, while poetic, do not always lend themselves to *immediate* ease of interpretability and usability in the context of evaluation. While House (1980) unpacks these terms in his book, *Evaluating with Validity*, it has not always been entirely clear why these particular terms were chosen and what sparked their emergence within House's writing. We now know that truth, beauty, and justice were substituted for credibility, coherence, and justice as fairness, respectively, and that the substitutes were suggested to House by Keats' "Ode on a Grecian Urn" to add literary flair. More importantly, we also now know that all three of these terms were "based on . . . early evaluation experiences and grew organically from the center outward, a piece at a time as [House] encountered specific problems" (House, Chapter 1 in this issue, p. 10). Some of these practical problems were field-based; for example, the Illinois Gifted Education Program evaluation sparked both the justice and beauty components of House's framework. Other practical problems were rooted in the dominant scholarship of the time concerning arguments about how best to define, demarcate, and establish validity (e.g., Campbell & Stanley, 1963; Cook & Campbell, 1979; Cronbach & Associates, 1980; Cronbach & Meehl, 1955; Scriven, 1972), and that these debates served as the foundation for the truth dimension of his framework.

Another clarity-of-language issue emerged as the preparation of the current NDE issue unfolded. As we reviewed draft chapters, we observed that some of our contributors were using *different* underlying definitions of the word credibility, particularly as it related to the truth and beauty dimensions of House's framework. As others (Barela, 2005; Christie, 2003; Christie & Rose, 2003) have highlighted, instances of inconsistent word stocks within our evaluation lexicon can be found; for example, the ways in which the term justice is defined and enacted from a deliberative democratic (House & Howe, 1999) as compared to an empowerment

(Fetterman, 2001) perspective. With House's assistance, in the second interview we sought to bring greater clarity to credibility, as a means to better inform the translation of this concept into practice.

James: How do you see credibility being connected across the beauty and truth dimensions?

Ernie: I'm guessing whatever I said in those papers was probably a bit confusing. So, let's say you do something such as I talk about in one of those papers; what Joseph Gusfield (1976) did with the drunk driver studies. He took a bunch of studies on drinking and driving, put them together, and ended with a new image of drunk drivers. It turns out people were thinking about individuals who were drinking and driving as being social drinkers—they go to a cocktail party, have a couple drinks, drive home, and get picked up by the police. The studies Gusfield reviewed changed the image of the drunk driver to one of a falling down drunk. So, now you have this image, which holds the whole thing together in a vivid way. It's very believable, highly credible if you bought into the image, and the image acted coherently to hold that together.

You could conceivably look at the studies Gusfield reviewed and see if they really supported the idea of the drinking driver as being a falling down drunk. *If that were not the case*, using the image in that way would be inappropriate. And that would be an invalid conclusion about those studies.

Looking at studies of Celebrex, the arthritis drug, provides another example. You could look at the studies and say these are double-blinded and randomized studies. You might therefore conclude that they would be credible. That is, until you looked deeply into the studies themselves, and you find what they've actually done inside the studies invalidates them.

If you want to test the truth of the study, whether it's really valid or not, you have to look in great detail at the studies themselves. We don't do that most of the time and we probably should. We look at stuff from afar and say, it looks like it's probably all right. We usually don't have any reason to go into it.

The exception to this is with high profile meta-evaluations. I've done about a half-dozen of them. I actually had a reason to look closer because somebody asked me to go into the internal workings of the studies and see how good the studies were, whether the findings, which got great publicity, were really true or not. That's when you put it to the real test, when you have the professional community taking a look up close.

So, from afar, that's how I think about credibility. And, validity is more than credibility because it's a deeper inspection of the study by the professional community. The deeper inspection is critical.

James: It sounds like you are actually talking about two different senses of credibility. In one sense, credibility in the beauty dimension, which lends itself to face validity. And, in another sense, credibility in the truth dimension has to do with talking to your stakeholders about what kinds of evidence they would find credible as you strive to produce this valid, true study.

Ernie: I'm not sure it is different. I'm not sure it isn't the same kind of credibility. You are looking at what means something to people. You are looking at the image of the drinking driver, and you've actually got a situation where the drinking driver image carries a lot of weight. It's the way people understand the world. Right? And it carries a lot of credibility just because it is such a powerful image. I'm not sure that it is different.

James: In the truth chapter you spent a lot of time talking about credibility. Can you say more about that?

Ernie: It's important to remember that what I was doing in the truth chapter was responding to the context at the time. We still had strong positivist influences in evaluation. Within the larger social science community, we still had a strong empiricist philosophy in the "foundations" view that argued that we were still going to find the truth of this stuff at the very bottom. I was pushing off, arguing against that by talking about nonfoundational conceptions of truth and validity. I think that's where credibility got placed in that argument. That is, we will never know for certain whether things are true; we don't have a way of determining certain things. I probably used it without thinking about the concept itself.

Some years later, I wrote the paper on credibility and coherence. At that time, I was more interested in the coherence concept—constructing things; putting things all together somehow.

Enduring Issues in Validity in Evaluation

One of the issues House discussed in his original book was the idea of naming and framing. According to Schön and Rein (1995), naming and framing are part of any problem-setting process. Schön (1983) argues that, "problem setting is a process in which, interactively, we name the things to which we will attend and frame the context in which we will attend to them" (p. 40). Further, it is through this process of naming and framing, often grounded in a powerful metaphor, that "stories make the 'normative leap' from data to recommendations, from fact to values, from 'is' to 'ought'" (Schön & Rein, 1995, p. 26). In trying to tease apart credibility from the truth and beauty perspectives, House's original ideas around naming and framing within the context of evaluation resurfaced. While this conversation relates back to clarity of language, it's also rooted in what House perceives as one enduring issue in evaluating with validity.

NEW DIRECTIONS FOR EVALUATION • DOI: 10.1002/ev

James: Based on my own experiences, the way you are using credibility in the context of the truth dimension almost seems to me like *plausible*, which has a different flavor than credibility from the beauty dimension. For example, when I say something is plausible as opposed to being valid on prima facie, it means that I'm starting to see you've got some good thinking and reasoning there. Whether or not it's true, I cannot say.

Ernie: Well, those are closely connected. And, as you've said, they are not exactly the same thing. You carry the image, and a lot of credibility, through images that you are not even aware of. For example, underlying the backbone of the Rossi, Freeman, and Wright (1979) textbook is actually an extended metaphor of the assembly line and pipeline. They don't say that, but if you read it, they use that imagery all the time. This was the old edition, but it's probably still true of the new Rossi, Lipsey, and Freeman (2004) edition. Anyway, if you look at the old edition, there's a pipeline image. If you read the book that way, you start looking at things that way without knowing it. For example, how tight are the objectives, how tightly are the activities tied to the objectives, etcetera. You follow that track implicitly based on this pipeline structure. And you probably would not be aware of that as an evaluator, unless you are acutely aware of the metaphors you are reading that are sunk in the book itself.

So you could be influenced by that and start looking at how the program is articulated. Now this is not just idle thought because that's the kind of evaluation applied to Jesse Jackson's PUSH Excel program. Was it tightly orchestrated? Was it tightly articulated? It didn't have objectives that you could reach. It was a church program where people had a "together" experience. And they got motivated. Well, that's nothing like a pipeline. That's nothing like a tightly orchestrated program, which is what evaluators applied to it.

Bianca: I think you talk a little about this in your own chapter in this NDE issue. In that chapter, you put it in terms of how you frame things and the frames we bring.

Ernie: Exactly. Some framing is implicit where you don't realize you're framing it that way. And some frames you're explicit about. It's better to know what you're using as the frame. The framing is very important. I'm more aware of the framing than I was thirty years ago when I wrote those articles. I've got a clearer picture now.

Human beings make sense of stuff by framing. You can't make sense out of it without framing it. Making sense out of it means framing it. But you can use frames that are better, and you can use frames that are worse. That's the idea. And that's where you get into coherence and credibility. It seems reasonable to me to use those criteria because you've already framed it a certain way.

The original ideas presented in *Evaluating With Validity* around "naming and framing" have been legitimated by cognitive psychology. The cognitive researchers have done empirical studies that suggest that you can't understand things without a story. That was also true back then. Writers and those with a little literary background have always known that. I'm not sure whether our understanding is any better. But the ideas have more legitimacy now that they didn't have when the book was originally published.

Bianca: Related to this conversation, are our own cognitive biases in terms of how we frame and think about evaluation an enduring issue?

Ernie: That's right. One enduring issue is cognitive bias. And biases are a productive way to think about evaluation because biases are remedial. You might be able to correct biases.

"Biased" may be too strong, but you frame things a certain way and not another way. For example, Hopson and Hood have highlighted biases related to culture. You've got those kinds of biases, which certainly do exist.

Bianca: As a means to help us become more reflective and aware of our cognitive biases, are there other examples that illustrate the ways cognitive bias might creep in unintentionally?

Ernie: Another thing the field must contend with is social class bias. Most people working in evaluation come from middle class backgrounds. And they see the world in a middle class way, which is a certain way to see the world. Yet, a lot of programs that we evaluate are for the poor and the powerless, those not at the middle or top of society. Because the evaluators come from the same education background and social class as the sponsors, they identify with the sponsors, or with the people who are delivering the programs. It's natural to do that. Sometimes that creates some biases, vis-à-vis, some of the people that are actually working with the programs themselves. That's a bias that we rarely talk about in evaluation.

Bianca: It's interesting that you would say that because I tend to think of Bledsoe's (Chapter 6 in this issue) work in community-based evaluation and Mertens' (2009) work in transformative evaluation as attending very much to issues, such as class, power, and inclusion.

Ernie: Right. Exactly. Katrina Bledsoe's paper in this issue is very good along those lines. But cognitive biases in evaluation are underexposed in general. And a whole family of biases relating to social class probably should be exposed. That brings us to the question of how to counter the biases.

As a first step you have to develop a story, an overall story of what happened, and whether the story is any good. If you come from the middle class background I alluded to, you would tend to develop a story that would fit middle class thinking. As opposed to how people in the lower social orders might see things. So, you end up with different interpretations and will likely neglect other interpretations, because of how you see the world. This is why it's important to talk to people up and down the social structure in which you're engaged rather than just talking to sponsors and a few key program people. If you only do the latter, you are going to get, I would say, a biased or narrow view of what the program is and what's going on in the program. There are ways to counter the biases.

New Directions for Evaluating With Validity

While we discussed future directions for extending House's framework in the context of evaluation practice, it was difficult to separate new directions from enduring issues. Enduring issues are omnipresent because they are grounded in fundamental issues in evaluation (e.g., values, validity, and truth). It follows then that it's unlikely that we will ever arrive at some agreed upon place; that is, unequivocally solve the big issues in the field. More likely is a nuanced, and different understanding, and thereby discussion of, these issues. In looking at the chapters included in the present issue, and in speaking with House, it is clear that these discussions are influenced by a number of factors, including changing contexts rooted in values, beliefs, and norms.

> Bianca: Can you talk about how your framework and the ideas it represents help us move forward as a field in terms of evaluating with validity?

> Ernie: Some concepts and ideas are about fundamental issues—values, biases, justice, coherence, validity, etcetera. But as the social context changes, we keep having new issues emerge.

> For example, back in the sixties, seventies, and eighties, conflict of interest for evaluators did not seem to be important. But the social context has changed. And now, because of structural changes in the society itself, we have a new set of potential biases, a family of biases that we have to deal with, or should deal with. As you know I've been interested in conflict of interest. And there are other issues. The politics of evaluation will always be there, for example, but the politics change.

> Of course, a lot of these things are outside our control. When society changes in a way that promotes conflict of interest, it's really outside the evaluator's control. All we can really do is react to it when it happens.

> Further, you can't find every conceivable bias. If you start listing all the biases you could actually think about, that list would be endless. So you have to pick the biases that seem to be the most threatening to the validity of the evaluations themselves. Again, those threats change with the social context. There will always be new issues coming forth because the social context changes.

> For example, I noticed this year the theme of the European Evaluation Society (EES) is "Evaluation for an Equitable Society." Equity has somehow come to the consciousness of EES. Equity has always been an issue, but now it is pushing to the forefront. It's not that we suddenly have inequality where we

didn't have it before. It's just that it wasn't seen as a big problem as it is now. Inequality has increased quite a bit and is increasing. You can see evaluation getting involved in that. Somehow that will play into the stuff we will be talking about over the next five to ten years. And it will play out in different ways.

Usually, as I said in talking about the origin of the ideas in *Evaluating With Validity*, I encountered a practical problem. I went to other fields and thought through how I might address this problem in evaluation by taking stuff from politics, philosophy, literary theory, or economics. I tried to address it that way. Sometimes the ideas coming in become the new ideas in the field that you're in.

Concluding Thoughts

What implications result from the ideas contained in this NDE issue for evaluation practice and theory, both presently and in the future? An underlying theme present throughout much of the proceeding discussion is the importance of context in evaluation. This is not a novel concept. Attending to context is a major component of many formal evaluation theories (e.g., Patton, 2010; Stufflebeam & Shinkfield, 2007; Weiss, 1997) and the subject of studies on evaluation (e.g., Azzam, 2010; Greene, 2001; Rog, Fitzpatrick, & Conner, 2012; Taut & Alkin, 2003). However, what was innovative, and continues to be of great importance to the field of evaluation, is that the framework proposed by House (1980) provides a schema to assist us in attending to important aspects of validity in an ever-evolving context.

As highlighted by Alkin (1991), one factor that influences the development of evaluation theory, and by extension folk theory,[1] are field-based experiences. The challenges confronted in the contexts in which we practice give birth to innovations in the theory and practice of evaluation. Thus, what this NDE issue offers is not only an indication of the current context grounded in House's validity framework but also illustrations of what pieces of context our chapter contributors believe are important to attend to, how they are attempting to attend to them, and what values they bring to bear in doing so. Griffith and Montrosse-Moorhead highlight the importance of attending to truth, coherence, and credibility. Davidson, Hurteau and Williams, and Azzam and Levine are most concerned with challenges related to the beauty dimension of House's framework. Yet they approach it from different perspectives. Davidson is keenly attuned to what she perceives as problems with coherence and credibility. Hurteau and Williams are concerned with the production of credible judgments. And Azzam and Levine call attention to the intersection of politics and credibility. Finally, both Bledsoe and Hopson continue to advocate for the importance of the justice dimension. Bledsoe approaches this conversation from a community-based evaluation perspective, while Hopson continues to advance arguments about the position of justice in our formal evaluation theories.

In addition, the present chapter attempts to clarify the meaning of credibility. Through this process, we have come to agree with House that there aren't necessarily two senses of credibility, but rather two or more things that contribute to credibility. Just as truth and beauty both contribute to validity, we also believe that both contribute to credibility. Beauty contributes to credibility in the sense that it creates, or places the evidence within, a picture that gives the evidence meaning for the audience(s). If the story or metaphor does not resonate with stakeholders, if the problem is not set in a way that stakeholders readily understand, they are not likely to find the evaluation credible. Meanwhile, truth contributes to credibility, by offering evidence that makes sense, or is acceptable, to the audience, particularly within the picture painted by beauty.

Further, though House does not explicitly call attention to it, an argument could be made that justice also contributes to credibility. That is, when stakeholder voices are omitted, particularly those who have been historically underrepresented or excluded altogether, this also impinges upon credibility. In this NDE issue, Bledsoe provides support for this position in her discussions of communities either disengaging from work with outsiders or taking a more active role in the evaluation process. Hopson provides another example in the context of formal evaluation theories and the use of decolonizing methodologies in evaluation practice. And, House implicitly alludes to this during the interviews when he discusses social classes bias.

In closing and in presenting the ideas in the issue, we have been careful not to offer another prescriptive model or theory of evaluation or a series of discrete, sequential steps. Rather, we hope readers of this issue will walk away with deeper understandings of House's framework and the components within as well as how the framework and its constituent parts can assist in establishing an evaluations' validity.

Note

1. As Christie and Rose (2003) point out, folk theory is distinct from formal evaluation theory. Folk theory recognizes that "human beings do not act without some kind of belief or assumption about what they are doing, which in essence is an implicit theory" (p. 41). They go on to argue that this implicit theory, or folk theory, is what guides the assumptions, beliefs, and behaviors of evaluation practitioners not formally trained in evaluation.

References

Alkin, M. C. (1991). Evaluation theory development II. In M. McLaughlin & D. Phillips (Eds.), *Evaluation and education at quarter century* (pp. 91–112). Chicago: University of Chicago Press.

Azzam, T. (2010). Evaluator stakeholder responsiveness. *American Journal of Evaluation*, *31*, 45–65. doi:10.1177/1098214009354917

Barela, E. (2005, October). *How school district evaluators make sense of their practice: A folk theory*. Paper presented at the joint conference of the Canadian Evaluation Society and the American Evaluation Association, Toronto, Ontario, Canada.

Campbell, D. T., & Stanley, J. (1963). *Experimental and quasi-experimental designs for research*. Chicago, IL: Rand-McNally.

Christie, C. A. (2003). Understanding evaluation theory and its role in guiding practice: Formal, folk, and otherwise. In C. A. Christie (Ed.), *New Directions for Evaluation: No. 97. The practice–theory relationship in evaluation* (pp. 91–93). San Francisco, CA: Jossey-Bass. doi:10.1002/ev.79

Christie, C. A., & Rose, M. (2003). The language of evaluation theory: Insights gained from an empirical study of evaluation theory and practice. *The Canadian Journal of Program Evaluation*, *18*, 33–45.

Cook, T. D., & Campbell, D. T. (1979). *Quasi-experimentation: Design and analysis issues for field settings*. Boston, MA: Houghton Mifflin.

Cronbach, L. J., & Associates (1980). *Toward reform of program evaluation*. San Francisco, CA: Jossey-Bass.

Cronbach, L. J., & Meehl, P. E. (1955). Construct validity in psychological tests. *Psychological Bulletin*, *52*, 281–302. doi:10.1037/h0040957

Fetterman, D. M. (2001). *Foundations of empowerment evaluation*. Thousand Oaks, CA: Sage.

Greene, J. C. (2001, November). *Introduction to the panel on understanding evaluators' practice decisions: The influence of theory, philosophy, values, experience, and individuality*. Paper presented at the Annual AEA Conference, St. Louis, MO.

Gusfield, J. (1976). The literary rhetoric of science: Comedy and pathos in drinking driver research. *American Sociological Review*, *41*, 16–34. doi:10.2307/2094370

House, E. R. (1980). *Evaluating with validity*. Beverly Hills, CA: Sage.

House, E. R., & Howe, K. R. (1999). *Values in evaluation and social research*. Thousand Oaks, CA: Sage.

Keats, J. (1909). Ode on a Grecian Urn. In E. de Selincourt (Ed.), *The poems of John Keats* (pp. 194–195). Retrieved from http://books.google.com/books?id=h6I/AAAAYAAJ&dq=ode+on+a+grecian+urn+by+john+keats&lr=&source=gbs˙navlinks˙s (Original work published 1820)

Mertens, D. M. (2009). *Transformative research and evaluation*. New York, NY: Guilford Press.

Patton, M. Q. (2010). *Developmental evaluation: Applying complexity concepts to enhance innovation and use*. New York, NY: Guilford Press.

Rog, D. J., Fitzpatrick, J. L., & Conner, R. F. (Eds.). (2012). *New Directions for Evaluation: No. 135. Context: A framework for its influence on evaluation practice*. San Francisco, CA: Jossey-Bass.

Rossi, P. H., Freeman, H. E., & Wright, S. R. (1979). *Evaluation: A systematic approach* (1st ed.). London, UK: Sage.

Rossi, P. H., Lipsey, M. W., & Freeman, H. E. (2004). *Evaluation: A systematic approach* (7th ed.). Thousand Oaks, CA: Sage.

Schön, D. A. (1983). *The reflective practitioner: How professionals think in action*. New York, NY: Basic Books.

Schön, D. A., & Rein, M. (1995). *Frame reflection: Toward the resolution of intractable policy controversies*. New York, NY: Basic Books.

Scriven, M. (1972). Objectivity and subjectivity in educational research. In L. Thomas (Ed.), *Philosophical redirection of educational research* (71st Yearbook of the NSSE; pp. 94–142). Chicago, IL: National Society for the Study of Education.

Stufflebeam, D. L., & Shinkfield, A. J. (2007). Daniel Stufflebeam's CIPP model for evaluation: An improvement/accountability approach. In D. L. Stufflebeam & A. J. Shinkfield (Eds.), *Evaluation theory, models, and applications* (pp. 325–366). San Francisco, CA: Wiley.

Taut, S., & Alkin, M. (2003). Program staff perceptions of barriers to evaluation implementation. *American Journal of Evaluation, 24*, 213–226. doi:10.1177/109821400302400205

Weiss, C. H. (1997). *Evaluation: Methods for studying programs and policies* (2nd ed.). Englewood Cliffs, NJ: Prentice-Hall.

BIANCA MONTROSSE-MOORHEAD is an assistant professor in the Measurement, Evaluation and Assessment Program, a research scientist for the Collaborative on Strategic Education Reform (CSER), and coordinator of the Graduate Certificate Program in Program Evaluation at the University of Connecticut.

JAMES C. GRIFFITH is a doctoral candidate for a dual degree in philosophy and psychology at the Claremont Graduation University and a lead evaluator at the Claremont Evaluation Center.

PAMELA POKORNY is a doctoral student in the Measurement, Evaluation, and Assessment Program at the University of Connecticut.

INDEX

ORDER FORM SUBSCRIPTION AND SINGLE ISSUES

DISCOUNTED BACK ISSUES:

Use this form to receive 20% off all back issues of *New Directions for Evaluation*.
All single issues priced at **$23.20** (normally $29.00)

TITLE	ISSUE NO.	ISBN

*Call 888-378-2537 or see mailing instructions below. When calling, mention the promotional code JBNND
to receive your discount. For a complete list of issues, please visit www.josseybass.com/go/ev*

SUBSCRIPTIONS: (1 YEAR, 4 ISSUES)

☐ New Order   ☐ Renewal

U.S.	☐ Individual: $89	☐ Institutional: $334
CANADA/MEXICO	☐ Individual: $89	☐ Institutional: $374
ALL OTHERS	☐ Individual: $113	☐ Institutional: $408

*Call 888-378-2537 or see mailing and pricing instructions below.
Online subscriptions are available at www.onlinelibrary.wiley.com*

ORDER TOTALS:

Issue / Subscription Amount: $ _____

Shipping Amount: $ _____
(for single issues only – subscription prices include shipping)

Total Amount: $ _____

SHIPPING CHARGES:	
First Item	$6.00
Each Add'l Item	$2.00

*(No sales tax for U.S. subscriptions. Canadian residents, add GST for subscription orders. Individual rate subscriptions must
be paid by personal check or credit card. Individual rate subscriptions may not be resold as library copies.)*

BILLING & SHIPPING INFORMATION:

☐ **PAYMENT ENCLOSED:** *(U.S. check or money order only. All payments must be in U.S. dollars.)*

☐ **CREDIT CARD:**   ☐ VISA   ☐ MC   ☐ AMEX

Card number _____ Exp. Date _____

Card Holder Name _____ Card Issue # _____

Signature _____ Day Phone _____

☐ **BILL ME:** *(U.S. institutional orders only. Purchase order required.)*

Purchase order # _____
      Federal Tax ID 13559302 • GST 89102-8052

Name _____

Address _____

Phone _____ E-mail _____

Copy or detach page and send to: **John Wiley & Sons, One Montgomery Street, Suite 1200,
San Francisco, CA 94104-4594**

Order Form can also be faxed to: **888-481-2665**

PROMO JBNND